EXPLORING THE EARTH

EXPLORING THE EARTH

I. O. EVANS
F.R.G.S.

illustrated by
WILLIAM McLAREN

HUTCHINSON OF LONDON

HUTCHINSON & CO. (*Publishers*) LTD
178–202 Great Portland Street, London, W.1

London Melbourne Sydney
Auckland Bombay Toronto
Johannesburg New York

★

First published 1961

*This book has been set in Baskerville type face. It has
been printed in Great Britain by The Anchor Press,
Ltd., in Tiptree, Essex, on Antique Wove paper and
bound by Taylor Garnett Evans & Co., Ltd., in
Watford, Herts*

ACKNOWLEDGMENTS

The author's thanks are due to the Library Staff of the Royal Geographical Society for their help, and to Mr. Patrick Moore, F.R.A.S., for his kindness in reading and criticizing the text of this book.

Contents

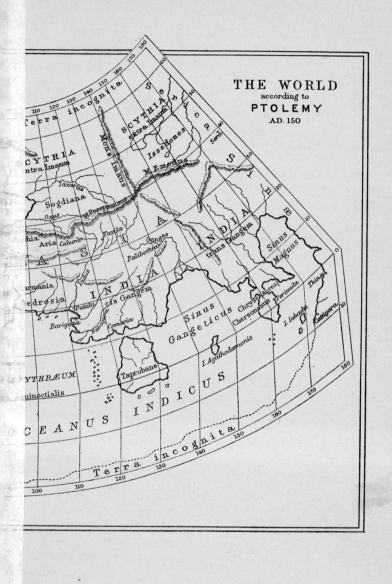

THE WORLD
according to
PTOLEMY
A.D. 150

INTRODUCTION

'We were dreamers, dreaming greatly, in the man-stifled town,
We yearned towards the skyline where the strange roads go down.'

WE HAVE all felt that yearning, which Kipling describes so well in his stirring poem. Few of us are ever
able to respond to it: first we have our education to get
and then our living to earn.

To some, however, that yearning is irresistible: they
cannot bear to live in the man-stifled town or even in
the familiar countryside; they have to cross that skyline
to see what lies beyond. Such as these become explorers
who face untold hardships crossing unknown regions
by land or sea, or in modern times by air; later they
may be the spacemen, braving unpredictable perils in
distant worlds.

Here is a brief record of what some of the explorers
have achieved. So numerous are they that only a com-
parative few can be mentioned; countless others have
had to be omitted to keep the record from becoming too
much a list of persons and places and dates. Because it
has to be brief, not much can be said of any, just enough
to tell you who they were, what they achieved, what
perils and difficulties they faced; and, most interesting

11

of all, perhaps, just what motive it was that urged them on their way, and why they went where they did instead of somewhere else.

Their motives were as varied as the experiences they encountered. Some were seeking adventure, some seeking fame, and others seeking loot; some were looking for new trade-routes, markets, or sources of raw materials for industry; some wished to serve their country by increasing its power or prestige; some aimed at advancing science; some devoted their lives to spreading their religious faith. But all had that eager desire to know, far different from mere idle curiosity, which drove them to find what lay beyond that skyline and whither those strange roads led.

Those who seriously wish to become explorers need not give up the idea as hopeless, for in these stirring times nobody quite knows where life will take him. Some would-be adventurers, indeed, have actually been selected for inclusion in Polar expeditions largely because in addition to their other qualifications they had shown prowess as King's or Eagle Scouts.

Exploration demands much more than health and strength and undaunted courage; more even than experience in mountaineering or caving or handling small boats. In these days, whatever its ultimate aim, every exploration has to be scientific, and members of teams are chosen largely on account of their technical knowledge. For this reason a schoolboy who starts by collecting fossils or being curious about the lie of the rocks may study geology seriously, take it up as a profession, and join in a quest for oil or uranium in distant countries as yet very imperfectly mapped.

Those of us who can never share in the hardships or triumphs of the explorers can sympathize with the one and rejoice in the other. We can be stirred by the record of their achievements, whether these ended in success or in glorious failure: we can understand the excitement of Hillary and Tenzing as they reached the wind-swept summit of Everest, or be moved by the final entry in the diary of Captain Scott.

We all enjoy stories of adventure, and the narratives of the great explorations describe feats more exciting than the fantastic doings of the characters in Westerns and thrillers—with the additional advantage that they are not fictional, but real.

As you read these stories, you will find it almost essential to follow the routes of the explorers on the maps in your atlas, and helpful too to consult a globe of the earth. The very wording on those maps and that globe will recall mighty achievements, in the names of island and headland, of bay and strait, called after those who first saw them rising over the horizon or looming dimly out of the Arctic mists.

I.O.E.

1 Early Exploration

FROM the earliest times many voyages were made into the unknown, but in many of the records of these adventures fact and fiction are so strangely blended that it is hard to know the truth. Exploration is far older than civilization, for right from prehistoric days people have had to find somewhere to live.

Hardly had the Great Ice Age passed away and the climate become warmer than tribes of hunters found their way into Southern Europe. They were great travellers, for they used to rally every year at a place now called Solutré, in Eastern France; and some of them roamed further afield into the heart of England— one of the animal drawings they delighted in making was found, scratched on a fragment of bone, at Creswell in Derbyshire.

The earliest explorers crossed the seas in simple boats or canoes or rafts and penetrated deep into unknown lands, until at last much of the world was inhabited by primitive peoples.

When, maybe fifteen thousand years ago, civilization began, explorers spread it far and wide; westward into Ireland, eastward through India to the coasts of China, southward into Africa, and across the ocean into Central America.

The beginnings of civilization may have occurred in Egypt, for here the Nile floods and its waters subside just at the right time to make the corn grow; or possibly in Mesopotamia, now called Iraq—the region, according to the Bible, where man was created—or in both. Civilization also developed in the great river valleys of India and China, and in Yucatán and Mexico and Peru.

The civilized people were brownish or 'dark white'— not negroid, but certainly not fair-skinned. Unlike the primitive peoples, they were not just food-collectors, but were food-producers: instead of picking nuts and berries they *grew* corn, and instead of merely being hunters they were shepherds and herdsmen. They could weave and make pottery, and lived not in rock-shelters and tents, but in wooden huts or in houses built of brick or stone. They made weapons not only for hunting, but also for war.

Their religion seems to have been a form of sun-worship, carried out in great stone circles or beside great stone monuments. Hence they are said to belong to the Heliolithic Culture, from the Greek words for 'sun' and 'stone'.

Their greater knowledge and superior weapons enabled them to master the primitive races, to civilize them and teach them their ways, and to become their rulers. These conquerors might even be regarded as 'gods'—a magic superhuman people, the Children of the Sun.

Some of these masterful explorers were looking for new lands where the growing populations could live. Some, perhaps, wanted to conquer and rule. Some were simply restless and adventurous and unable to settle down. Others desired to find useful metals or ornamental materials such as gold or precious stones. Others again were intent on a more important quest: they believed that somewhere in the world there existed a happy land where nobody ever grew old, where they would find things which would make their owners immortal: they sought the Islands of the Blessed, for the Fountain of Youth, and for the magical Givers of Life.

They never found them, and soon travel and exploration became more commonplace and matter-of-fact, its purpose being new colonies and trade. The early civilizations imported raw materials and exported manufactured goods as nations do today. Merchants shipped their wares abroad in large cargo-vessels, and to protect them against pirates and trade-rivals they built swift, well-armed warships. Then, as now, the nations sought 'command of the sea'.

Some of the earliest vessels shown on the Egyptian paintings are quite large, propelled partly by sails and partly by oars. Greek writers say that 'Nanaus the Egyptian invented fifty-oared ships', and the Egyptian hieroglyph (picture-word) for 'ships' was simply a crude drawing of a square sail. With such a sail, ships could only drive before a favourable wind: they could not tack obliquely into the wind like modern sailing-ships. They were not very rigid, and to prevent their 'hogging' (rising amidships), their prow and stern had to be braced together with stout cables. Probably they began as river-boats on the Nile, and were adapted, maybe about five thousand years ago, for use at sea.

Yet with such boats the Egyptians could make remarkable voyages; to Phoenicia for timber, and right down the Red Sea to Punt (now called Somaliland) or South Arabia for incense, needed in temple worship.

About 1500 B.C. an expedition went to Punt. So that she might adorn her temple with living incense-trees, Queen Hatshepsut sent five large sailing-ships with goods for barter up the Nile, through a canal, and down the Red Sea. They returned laden with 'the wonders of Punt, such as had never before been seen': incense, valuable timber, gold, ivory, and human slaves. Pictures of the ships show them piled high with bales of merchandise, the trees growing in their tubs, and baboons squatting about on the deck.

Command of the Mediterranean was held for many years by the Aegean or Minoan civilization with its centre at Crete. Under its king, whose legendary title was Minos, its people explored and founded colonies on the shores of the Aegean Sea—hence its other name— and traded with Egypt, over three hundred miles away. We do not know as much about this civilization as we should like, for its writing has not yet been fully de- ciphered; but the engravings on its seals show its large powerful ships, propelled by oars and sails. There is a Greek legend that the engineer Daedalus made arti- ficial wings on Crete, and this may simply be a poetic manner of saying that it was there that sails were first invented.

So powerful was their navy that the Cretans did not trouble to fortify their capital, Cnossos: they relied on their 'wooden walls'. These indeed protected them for about fifteen hundred years, during which their civil- ization advanced tremendously and developed many refinements. Then, about 1400 B.C. Cnossos was looted, and the great Aegean civilization collapsed.

Command of the sea then passed from the Minoans to the Phoenicians, whose original trading-centres were Tyre and Sidon at the eastern end of the Mediterranean, and who founded colonies elsewhere on its shore. The greatest was Carthage on the African coast opposite Sicily; its explorers 'opened up' Africa for trade as far as the Sahara and cruised beyond the Pillars of Hercules (the Straits of Gibraltar) into the Atlantic, where they traded and founded colonies on the west coast of Spain.

So renowned were the Phoenician captains that the rulers of other lands were glad to employ them. The trade of King Solomon was carried on in the ships of Hiram, King of Tyre. When the ruler of the great Persian Empire wished to explore the northern coasts of the Mediterranean in the hope of conquering them, he hired Phoenician ships manned by experienced seamen from Sidon. In spite of their expeditions to Punt, the Egyptians were not seafaring people, and they permitted foreigners to handle their overseas trade. When about 600 B.C. Pharaoh Necho planned the most daring of all these explorations, it was Phoenician seafarers to whom he entrusted it.

The explorers set sail down the Red Sea and out into the ocean; autumn after autumn they landed on the African coast, sowed their corn and waited until it could be reaped, then set sail again. At last, having sailed right round Africa, they returned triumphantly, nearly three years later, through the Pillars of Hercules. They reported one strange fact which made the ancient thinkers doubt their accuracy, but which makes us inclined to believe them: they said that as they were sailing round Libya—the ancient name for Africa—they saw the noon sun in the north!

Other Phoenician traders made remarkable voyages. They traded regularly with the Tin Islands (probably the Scillies or Cornwall) and about 500 B.C. their captain Himilco put out into the Atlantic. For about four months his ships voyaged, largely through unknown waters, much hindered not only by fogs and calms and shoals, but also by masses of sea-weeds and inquisitive sea-monsters. This could mean that the ships had reached a shoal where sea-weeds grew thickly and tunny and whales were plentiful off Gades (now Cadiz) on the Spanish coast, but it is possible that they had entered the Sargasso Sea in the Western Atlantic. If so, by pushing on further westwards, Himilco might have discovered America.

Though Himilco and Pharaoh Necho's seamen must certainly have had exciting adventures, there is no record of them. But, fortunately, we have the log of another exploring expedition, made about the same time as that of Himilco, but in the opposite direction.

The merchants of Carthage sent Hanno, with a large fleet of ships and thousands of emigrants, to found colonies on the African coast. He founded several on the coast of Morocco and as far south as the Rio de Oro. Thence he made two explorations southward, the first as far as the mouth of a river infested with hippopotami and crocodiles, the Senegal, and the second to Macaulay Island, off Sierra Leone.

During their journey his crews were stoned by 'swarms of wild men in animal skins', and badly scared by the din of pipes and cymbals and tom-toms and howling, and the sight of countless bush fires. Towards the south the streams of fire from the blazing grass, sweeping before the wind, seemed to plunge into the sea; and flames also raged on a lofty mountain-top called the Chariot of the Gods.

An island the explorers landed on was inhabited by

savage people whose bodies were hairy and 'whom our interpreters called gorillas', but which were probably chimpanzees. They tried to capture some of these hairy people, but found them so fierce they had to kill them, taking their skins back to Carthage as a trophy. Though their nerve had been shaken by their adventures, Hanno and his men did not give up their quest until they found their food running short.

The Phoenicians, who lived by their trade, naturally did their utmost to keep others from sharing it. If they met a foreign vessel in their waters, they sank it and slaughtered or enslaved its crew. So determined were they that when one of their captains found a foreign ship shadowing him to the Tin Islands, he deliberately ran his own vessel on a sandbank, on which his pursuers also were wrecked. The rulers praised him for his self-sacrifice, and compensated him for the loss of his cargo.

In their attempts to keep off intruders, the Phoenicians even started a 'war of nerves', spreading horrific stories of the dangers which lay in wait for the unwary along the trade-routes.

2 Travellers' Tales

WHEN you read about the adventures of Sindbad the Sailor, or of some other legendary hero, do you ever wonder if such tales have any truth in them? How did such stories arise in the first place, and why have they had such a wide reading public for so many years?

Sindbad is said to have landed on what looked like a pleasant island, but was in fact an immense fish which had been asleep for so long that trees had sprouted from its back.

On yet another of his adventures he came across a gigantic white object which was the egg of a monstrous and terrifying bird called a 'Roc'. By lashing himself to one of the bird's legs, Sindbad escaped, to find himself in a valley, rich in precious stones, but guarded by venomous snakes.

During his travels his ship was attacked by an army of 'hairy folk like apes'; and when the crew were forced to land they were imprisoned by a man-eating giant. Though they succeeded in outwitting the monster, Sindbad was the only one who managed to escape, and to continue on his journey.

Sindbad was one type of legendary figure; some of the early Christian saints who did, in fact, really exist were also glorified in legend. It is easy to understand how around such brave and stalwart figures as, say, St. Patrick and St. Cuthbert, stories were told which added something to their reputation—even though the stories seem fantastic now. St. Brendan, for example, is said to have embarked on some truly remarkable voyages.

He was in search of 'The Island of the Blessed', and at last, we are told, he found it. In the bewildering mists which surrounded the pilgrims there suddenly appeared a brilliant light, and this revealed a land so clear and bright it seemed like Heaven. Its trees were laden with ripe fruit, but a mysterious voice warned the travellers not to cross the river which divided the island in two. Later the voice commanded them to return to their own land; so, taking all the fruit they could carry, they sorrowfully sailed away.

The greatest of all these legendary travels is described in the ancient epic poem, Homer's *Odyssey*. It describes the adventures of the Greek leader Odysseus (Ulysses in Latin), as, after taking part in the siege of Troy, he sought to return home. Helped by some of the gods, though hindered by others, he encountered a series of fantastic perils, some of which have been 'borrowed' by later story-tellers to retell about their own heroes.

Sindbad's encounter with the giant seems, for example, to be a retelling of Ulysses' escape from Polyphemus. Polyphemus was one of the Cyclops, a race of one-eyed giants; by first making him drunk and then burning out his eye, Ulysses succeeded in saving his crew and himself.

After an encounter with another race of giants, the crew were turned into swine by the enchantress Circe; but, helped by the god Hermes, Ulysses not only resisted her magic but induced her to turn the swine back into men. Later they had to pass rocks inhabited by the Sirens, sea-maidens who sing so charmingly that they lure passing seamen to run their ships on to the reefs; again Ulysses eluded their charm, though he was nearly driven frantic with longing to respond to it.

Then they had to traverse a narrow strait. Off one of its shores was Scylla, a many-armed monster the very sight of which was enough to alarm not only men but even the gods. Off its other shore was Charybdis, another monster, who alternately sucked down the sea and squirted it, foaming, back.

Though they escaped all these perils, the sailors of the crew were destroyed by a storm sent by an angry god, so that Ulysses was the only one to survive and return home. This part of the poem, though moving and exciting, involves no more contacts with monsters or giants or other inhuman beasts.

Another Greek legend, older even than the *Odyssey*, describes the cruise of the Argonauts, as under their leader Jason they went in search of the Golden Fleece. They too encountered many perils, including the 'clashing rocks' which would open as though to let a vessel pass and then suddenly close upon it and crush it: the good ship *Argo* did get safely through, but only just in time, for the tip of her stern was nipped and shorn off.

The oldest of all these stories is not Greek, but Egyptian. It relates that thousands of years ago a skipper sailed down the Red Sea on a trading voyage to the land of Punt. Though manned by a hundred skilled and courageous seamen, his vessel was wrecked in a sudden squall, and all the crew perished. The skipper himself seized a plank, and the waves washed him ashore on an unknown isle. This was no desert island, for it was rich in fruit and corn and herbs, in birds and fish; thankful for his deliverance, the shipwrecked mariner kindled a fire and offered sacrifice to the gods.

Suddenly he heard a thunderous noise, like the roar of the sea, which shook the trees and made the earth tremble. Fearfully uncovering his eyes, the skipper beheld a huge serpent, brilliantly coloured in gold and blue.

Unlike the sea-serpents of later legends, this princely creature was friendly and helpful. It assured the skipper that soon another vessel would arrive and take him on to Punt, where he would receive rich gifts to take home. The rescue-vessel duly came, and the skipper went back to Egypt in triumph, with a cargo of perfume, ornamental wood, ivory, and apes. Lest any other travellers should expect equal good fortune, he told them that after he left it that 'Island of the Blessed' had been swallowed up by the sea.

Naturally, we are no more inclined to believe in that benevolent sea-serpent than we are in Ulysses' one-eyed

Cyclops or in Sindbad's gigantic Roc! None the less, these stories tell us much about the world as it used to be, and serious historians have tried to think out the truths which may lie behind them. They have to make allowance, of course, for misunderstandings, and for the story-teller's natural wish to make his story sound both exciting and authentic.

The reason, in the Egyptian narrative, for mentioning that the island has vanished is easy to see—it is the sort of device by which a story-teller keeps his word from being doubted, explaining why no other traveller from Egypt to Punt had ever come across that wonderful island. (This device, you may have noticed, is sometimes used in various forms by modern fiction-writers.)

Some of the ancient stories may be sheer romancing: whoever made them up did so 'out of his own head', and the audience did not care whether they were true or not. We most of us enjoy a good 'wonder story'—that is why science fiction is so popular—and that was as true in ancient times as it is now. Although then the stories were told by word of mouth instead of in writing, people liked hearing about strange adventures and monsters in distant lands, just as we like reading about them in distant worlds.

It is very easy to misunderstand descriptions of creatures which one has never seen, and this may account for some details in these ancient stories and for the legends about fantastic beasts. A traveller might describe a rhinoceros as an animal something like a horse with one horn on its nose—and an artist hearing this and wanting to make his picture attractive might draw a unicorn.

Stories apart, people like believing that there are strange creatures in distant parts of the earth. Many of us would feel it rather a pity if we learned that there really is no such thing as the Loch Ness Monster or the sea-serpent, or if it were proved that the Yéti, the 'Abominable Snowman', a strange semi-human creature supposed to live in the Himalayas, is nothing more than a large mountain-bear. And how excited many of us would be if word came that an explorer had sighted a prehistoric monster in the tropics of Africa, or a mammoth in the Canadian North-West! Realizing that their audiences had such feelings, the ancient story-tellers naturally did their best to oblige them.

Even if it were proved that some weird creature or other did not actually live where people supposed, the legends about it went on. It was merely thought to live in some other land, further away or more difficult to reach, or maybe in some distant country which had never been explored.

There were other, more serious, reasons for stories of fierce monsters. Trade rivalries were as bitter then as they are now, and miners or owners of merchant ships wanted to keep a monopoly of the regions from which they got their wealth. So they tried to scare competitors away from the mines or the trade-routes by stressing the dangers they would have to face. Diamond-rich valleys, they said, were guarded by fearsome serpents such as those which Sindbad encountered; gold-mines by dragons or griffins or giant ants; and the oversea markets by monsters such as Scylla or Charybdis or by cannibalistic giants such as Polyphemus.

Yet even the wildest of legends may have some facts behind it. Just as when we read a space-travel story we like to harmonize with what is known about conditions on, say, the moon or Mars, so the ancient peoples expected the stories they heard to harmonize with what was really known about distant lands. Although the Egyptian story about the sea-serpent sounds like sheer romancing, the people who heard it knew that there was a country called Punt, with which Egypt carried on a profitable trade.

Similarly, the Arabs who enjoyed the *Arabian Nights* knew that there were lands with which Sindbad might well have traded, and the Greeks who enjoyed the *Odyssey* knew that there were places which might well be those which it mentions. Two thousand years ago the Greek thinkers were arguing about the facts behind their ancient poem, and the modern scholars are arguing about them still. Some of their attempts to explain these stories will be described in later chapters of this book.

One ancient legend has lasted so long that many people still believe that it may be true. That is the story about Atlantis, a great civilization said to have flourished long ago and to have been destroyed so completely that every trace of it has perished.

The story appears in two of the famous *Dialogues* of the Greek thinker Plato, who says that it was told, well before his time, to another Greek thinker by an Egyptian priest. It speaks of an immense island west of the 'Pillars of Hercules' (the Straits of Gibraltar) on which a powerful Empire ruled territories in North Africa and Western Europe. When it set out to conquer the rest of the earth there was only one city bold and well trained enough to withstand it and so to save the world from slavery. As Plato was an Athenian, it is not surprising to hear that that city was Athens! But then, the story continues, there were terrible earthquakes, in which the island of Atlantis was swallowed by the sea and vanished, leaving nothing but shoals of mud to mark the place where it had been.

In the *Dialogues* the civilization of Atlantis is described in great detail, with its mineral wealth and its rich forests, its herds of elephants and other animals, its canals and waterways and massive walls, its temple richly decorated with gold and silver and some mysterious metal called *orichalcum*, and its impressive ceremonies. But Zeus, the king of the gods, Plato tells us, wanted to punish its people for their sins; so having assembled the other gods he started to address them——

But here, most tantalizingly, the story breaks off, and what happened next we shall never know. Nor do we know, indeed, what Plato meant by his narrative. He may never have intended it to be taken seriously; he was fond of putting moral stories into his *Dialogues* to drive their lesson home, and his description of the fate of Atlantis, detailed though it is, may simply be one of them.

3 Fact or Fiction?

THERE were, however, seamen in the Mediterranean whom the Phoenicians could not frighten off; who were well able to look after themselves; and whose poets turned the 'horror stories' of strange monsters into stirring legends.

The Greeks were part of a race of fair-skinned warriors who travelled southwards through the Balkans, and conquered and took over its civilization. At first they were landsmen, knowing little of the sea, but they were quick-minded, adventurous, and ready to learn. They got their seamanship from the Phoenicians, and soon they were able to challenge them and to share in their trade.

31

It may have been the Greeks who destroyed the Aegean civilization. One of their legends relates that their hero Theseus sailed to Crete. There he slew a dreadful bull-headed monster, the Minotaur, who every year demanded a human sacrifice of Greek youths and girls. This legend may recall a time when the Greeks were subject to the Aegeans, and had to give some of their finest young people to be their slaves—until at last they revolted and themselves became the conquerors.

One of the oldest and finest of the world's great poems, Homer's *Iliad*, describes the siege of another Aegean city, Troy. This was long thought to be imaginary, but archæologists have found that Troy actually existed, and that it was destroyed and rebuilt several times. As this city, also called Hissarlik, commanded the entrance to the Dardanelles, its purpose may have been to levy tribute on traders plying between the Mediterranean and the Black Sea. And the merchants may have found it such a nuisance to their trade that they destroyed it time and again.

Some of the episodes in Homer's *Odyssey* may likewise be based on facts, especially when these had been 'touched up' by Phoenicians anxious to keep the Greeks out of the Western Mediterranean. The story of the Cyclops, the great one-eyed giant who tried to sink vessels by pelting them with rocks, may come partly from Mount Etna or some other volcano, towering up beside the shore like a giant, its crater blazing like a fiery eye and roaring and hurling boulders seaward. It may come partly from the bones of elephants and other large animals found on the shore of Sicily; even in fairly recent times such bones have been mistaken for those of giants, and since an elephant's skull has one large central opening, that of the nose, the Cyclops legend is easy to understand.

The legend of the Sirens, with their charming song, may simply mean that Homer, a blind poet, had heard the cries of the sea-birds and been told about that human-looking monster, the dugong.

Charybdis and Scylla may refer to the perils of the Straits of Gibraltar; the Phoenicians were especially anxious to scare other seamen away from this, for it was the route to the Tin Islands. The Strait is notorious for its high tides and dangerous whirlpools, and in its rock-crannies live octopi, whose arms, with their suckers, might easily be mistaken for heads bristling with teeth.

Homer's description of seamen transformed into swine by an enchantress may show that he knew what happens to some sailors when, at the end of a cruise, they reach a wineshop. But in the poem Ulysses gets them turned back into men (with a rope's end, perhaps?).

The land of the Kimmerians, said in the poem to be shrouded in mists and clouds and where the sun is never seen, sounds like the old joke about the English climate, especially as one of the tribes which formerly dwelt in Britain was the Cymry. Could this have been another Phoenician device for discouraging people from visiting the Tin Islands?

But not all the episodes in the *Odyssey* are horrific. Ulysses, it tells us, was befriended by the people of a

B

distant city (Plato may have had this story in mind when he described legendary Atlantis): so excellent were its ships that they needed no steersmen, as they could read the thoughts of the crews and find their way into harbour even in a fog. This may be a reference to the Aegean seamen, so skilled in navigation that they might well have been thought to have been using magic.

The legend of the quest of the Golden Fleece may similarly have been based on the exploits of some early explorers, though the poets who told it knew so little of geography that they got the details thoroughly mixed. Jason and the other Argonauts succeeded in traversing the Hellespont (the Dardanelles) and the Bosphorus, in spite of the strong winds and currents and eddies which make these straits so dangerous. Thus they reached the Black Sea, and at its eastern shores, in Colchis south of the Caucasus, Jason secured the Golden Fleece—some of the ancient geographers thought this got its name because the people of that land used woolskins to trap the gold-dust brought down by the mountain-streams.

Then, in some manner which the poet leaves vague, the Argonauts found themselves cruising off the Spanish coast; and at last, weather-beaten and weary, they reached home. During their voyage they may even have reached the Arctic, for the 'clashing rocks' episode may be a memory of some forgotten explorer who had a narrow escape among the icebergs.

The poems also tell us something of the methods sailors used in those ancient times. They understood the main points of the compass; when Ulysses was off an unknown coast, he complained ruefully that 'east and west mean nothing to us here'. Included in his gear was a long pole, used in the shallows to punt his ship along. At night he steered by the stars, the Pleiades and the brilliant star Arcturus as well as the Great Bear; and he also used the stars to get an idea of the time.

Finding the north by the Great Bear was not so easy then as it is now, for in those days there was no bright North Star conveniently near to the Pole. A slow movement of the earth's axis makes the north pole of the sky —the point round which the whole sky seems to revolve —move slowly in a small circle. When the Great Pyramid was built, a star named Thuban, in the Dragon, was near the Pole, but it had gradually moved away. Navigators had to notice the 'slant' of the Great Bear and to work out the direction of north by rather complicated rules. One of the things which the Phoenicians taught the Greeks was to find the north more accurately by observing the Little Bear, a star-pattern nearer the Pole, but fainter and more difficult to identify.

Whatever the truths behind their legends, the Greeks were as enterprising as the Phoenicians in seeking new sites for their colonies and new centres for their trade. Their cities in Greece soon got overcrowded; the greatest, Athens, was not self-supporting, but was as dependent as modern Britain on trade overseas. New homes simply had to be found for the growing populations by making settlements overseas: not colonies in our modern sense, governed from the homeland, but new independent city-states governing themselves.

Sometimes the priests of the Sun-god were consulted; they might even order a city to found a new colony, as when they told the King of Thera, an island in the Aegean, to found one in Libya (Africa).

The Therans were at first unwilling to obey, for they hardly knew where Libya was, and they dared not send colonists into the unknown. But a seven-year drought convinced them that the Sun-god meant business, and with some trouble they found a Cretan fisherman whom the winds had previously driven to Libya. So a shipload of colonists set out, landing not on the mainland but on an offshore island: a wise precaution in such circumstances, for the people on the mainland might have been hostile. Two further shiploads found the land so inhospitable that they returned home, but there the people hurled stones at them and drove them back. After staying on the island for some years they made friends with the mainland people, and so, about 640 B.C., they founded Cyrene.

One of the most westerly of the Greek colonies, Massilia, was founded more romantically. Sailors from Phocaea, pleased with the coast near the mouth of the Rhône, visited the local king, who at the time happened to be looking for a son-in-law. As was the custom in that tribe, his daughter was to choose her bridegroom at a banquet, and to this the king politely invited the foreign strangers; to his surprise the princess passed over the ordinary candidates and chose one of the Greeks.

Thus about 600 B.C. was founded what has become Marseilles, and soon it too was sending out expeditions to find sites for new colonies on the coast of Spain.

The Greeks were much more inquisitive and studious-minded than the other peoples. Not only did they systematically collect information about distant parts, but they also travelled in search of it.

One of the greatest Greek travellers was Herodotus, who in the fifth century B.C. set out on a mighty quest. The great Persian Empire had recently attempted to conquer the small city-states of Greece; though normally hostile to each other, these states had united to meet the challenge, and against all expectation they had defeated the invader by land and sea. Stirred by this victory, Herodotus devoted much of his life to describing the events which led up to it; and so great was the Persian Empire that this was rather like writing a history and geography of most of the known world.

To get his material he not only read deeply but travelled widely, from Babylon and Susa in Persia to Southern Italy, and from the north of the Black Sea to Egypt. By consulting records, visiting antiquities, studying ancient inscriptions, and consulting the priests and other knowledgeable people, he collected volumes of information. Naturally he also collected some faulty information, and made some errors, but in spite of these his *History* tells us much about the ancient world. It won him reward and honour, and it has always been valued not only by students but also by general readers. Though, of course, there had been earlier historians, Herodotus is called the 'Father of History' because he made it so interesting.

One of his narratives relates that when about 515 B.C. the Persian king wanted to annex 'India'—really the valley of the Indus—he sent a Greek officer to sail down the river. The explorer came back with glowing accounts of the country's wealth, but said that its gold was excavated in the deserts by giant ants, so dangerous that the only way for the gold-collectors to escape them was to sacrifice some of their camels. This may have been an Indian 'horror story' to keep trespassers away from the gold-diggings.

Travellers were willing to make long arduous journeys not only for history, but also for science. Pytheas of Masillia was a skilled mathematician anxious to explore the unknown, to describe distant lands and to study the ocean tides (the Mediterranean is almost tideless). Somehow, during the fourth century B.C., he dodged the Phoenician blockade at the Pillars of Hercules and sailed out into the Atlantic. From Gades he cruised up the coasts of Spain and France to Brittany.

He crossed to the Tin Islands, which he calls the Prettanic Islands—the origin of the name Britain—and Albion. He gives some details of the tin-mining, and says that the metal was shipped from an island called Ictis; as it was taken there in waggons at ebb-tide, this was plainly St. Michael's Mount.

He spent some time exploring Britain, estimated its shape and size, and collected much interesting information about its people and their way of life. He also mentions, and probably sighted, another large island to the west of Britain, which he called Ierne, and we call Ireland. He was impressed by the high tides off the British coast, having possibly seen a tidal race in Pentland Firth, and he refers to our 'extremely chilly climate'.

Returning to the Continent, he followed its coast beyond the Rhine to a river which he calls the Tanais, possibly the Elbe. Here, he says, live the Gutones (maybe the Teutons or Goths), who collect amber washed up on the shore of an island called Abalus, perhaps Heligoland. Beyond was a much larger land called Balcia, probably either Jutland or South Sweden. Then he returned along the coast to the Mediterranean, noticing that it was slower travelling in that direction—though he did not realize this, he had been helped on the northward journey by the Gulf Stream.

So astonishing were his discoveries that many of the thinkers disbelieved him; and what perplexed them most was his description of another land six days' sail beyond Britain—it is not clear whether he had visited it himself or merely heard about it. Here there were no proper crops, and no cattle; the inhabitants lived on wild berries and 'millet', which they had to thrash in barns because of the continual rain, and their drink was mead prepared from honey. Here, too, the nights were only two or three hours long, and here was a 'curdled sea' where nobody could either walk or sail. Pytheas compared it to a 'sea-lung', for it heaved as though some monster were breathing below the surface.

Unlikely though this sounded to the early geographers, the modern explorer Nansen said it was a very good description of the ice-sludge formed along the edge of the drift-ice ground to a pulp by the waves, and seen but dimly through the damp, grey Arctic mists. We cannot be sure, though, whether Thule, this northern country, was Iceland or part of the Norwegian coast.

4 Exploring Armies

THE great empires of old made conquests abroad, and had to know something about the lands they ruled. Their aim was not discovery, but victory and domination, and though they acquired much interesting information it was not for the sake of knowledge but as an aid to government, trade, and taxation. The Greek generals seem to have been the first to march notebook in hand and to publish studies of the regions through which they marched.

Though the Greek city-states had united to repel the Persians, they were soon again at war with one another. Their wars left them weakened, their trade badly crippled and their cities full of unemployed ex-service-

41

men, unable or unwilling to settle down to civil life, and ready to fight in foreign armies for pay.

Prince Cyrus, brother of Artaxerxes, Great King of Persia, raised an army of Greek mercenaries in order, he told them, to subdue some rebellious hillmen. Only when they had got well into Asia did they learn his real scheme: to overthrow the king and mount the throne. Such disloyalty horrified them, but he was able to overcome their scruples by raising their pay. So they marched on eastwards through Asia Minor and down the Euphrates almost to Babylon. Here, at the Battle of Cunaxa (401 B.C.), they met and defeated the forces of the Great King.

Then they learned, with dismay, that though they had won his battle for him, Prince Cyrus had been killed in the fighting. Thus that small Greek expeditionary force, only about ten thousand strong, found itself cut off far from home, in the heart of hostile country, surrounded by fierce enemies, and threatened by a vindictive king.

When their officers were treacherously murdered they completely lost heart, until a young Athenian 'soldier of fortune', Xenophon, rallied them and helped lead them through the unexplored regions north of the Euphrates (now Iraq and Armenia). They faced continual opposition, tough fighting, a shortage of supplies, and in the wintry mountains they had to contend with frostbite and snow-blindness. They lost their way, followed the wrong river, and had to retrace their steps.

At last their leaders were startled to hear a tremendous outcry from the vanguard. Fearing an enemy attack, they hastened forwards, and soon they too were joining in the mighty shout which arose from all the host:

'*Thalassa!*' ('The sea!')

More marching and fighting brought them to a friendly city on the shore of the Black Sea. Here they thankfully offered sacrifice to the gods, and held their regimental sports. In spite of further difficulties they found their way home to Greece.

So was accomplished the March of the Ten Thousand, which Xenophon, who in modern times would have made a good war-correspondent, described in his book, the *Anabasis* ('Up Country'). It makes exciting reading, and the information it gives about the lands they traversed has been very useful to geographers in ancient and modern times. Yet its greatest value was in showing the Greek-speaking world that the immense Persian Empire was ramshackle and unwieldy, and would yield to a determined attack.

The attack was made not by the Greeks themselves, but by a people to their north-west. The Macedonian king, Philip, had a large and well-trained army: after forcing the Greek cities to accept his leadership, he was planning the invasion of Persia when, in 336 B.C., he was assassinated.

His project was continued by his brilliant son

Alexander the Great. Having defeated the Persian armies in two desperate battles against heavy odds, the young king led his forces right through the Empire into the unknown regions beyond. Across the mountainous country south of the Caspian Sea, through a narrow pass called the Caspian Gates, east into Bactria, with a détour southwards, and then north-eastwards through Kandahar and Kabul, over the lofty mountains of the Hindu Kush to Samarkand, back to Kabul and through the Khyber Pass into India—they marched for years, in the face of continual difficulties and hardships and intermittent fighting.

Alexander would have pushed on even further, for he was reputed to have schemes for world conquest, but his soldiers were weary of this endless and seemingly aimless marching and fighting. Anxious to go home, they went on strike and refused to advance any further. Alexander's protests and entreaties were unavailing; so, bitterly disappointed, he had to return to Persia.

Sending his fleet back by sea, he led his army along the coast of the Indian Ocean, until the mountains made him turn inland. This sent them through very difficult and dangerous country, through barren deserts of rock and shifting sand where even the guides lost their way. Water ran short, and for lack of other food and fuel the troops had to eat the draught animals and burn the baggage-waggons; Alexander himself refused to ride and insisted on sharing his men's hardships. These were great indeed, but at last he reached Babylon.

Meantime his admiral, Nearchus, was leading his great fleet eastwards along the coast. Accustomed to the tideless Mediterranean, he and his men were confused by the tides; the natives were so hostile that he was unable to wait for the monsoon; and though his crews swam to safety, three of his ships were wrecked in a gale.

Nearchus had to commandeer supplies from the local natives, some of whom were clad in the skins of porpoises or whales, roofed their huts with turtle-shells, and, having no iron, killed fish and even split softwood with their finger-nails; their only weapons were wooden spears with tips hardened by burning, but these they used effectively enough. One island was so sacred that Nearchus was warned not to set foot on it, for those who did so vanished and were never heard of again. Undaunted, he proved the horror-story false by landing on the island himself, and discovered that it was the home of numerous fine turtles.

Astonished to see the ocean spurting like a whirl-wind, his sailors asked what it was; and when told it came from a school of whales they were so startled they dropped their oars. But Nearchus commanded them to advance in battle order. When they neared the whales they shouted loudly, blew their trumpets, and rattled their oars; whereupon the whales, as startled as the sailors were, vanished. Presently the spurting was seen again, but this time behind the fleet: the whales had swum beneath it.

Although he could not conquer the world, Alexander

did his best to unite the empire over which he ruled. But in 323 B.C. his untimely death, at the age of thirty-three, destroyed his plans, and the empire was divided among his generals.

Though he had conquered many people, destroyed many cities, and slain many enemies, Alexander was no mere blustering tyrant. He had founded new cities, encouraged trade, explored, and organized explorations. His tutor had been the great Greek philosopher Aristotle, who had given him a keen interest in science. Alexander appointed surveyors to pace out distances along the main traffic routes, and among his companions were skilled observers who studied the regions he traversed, their plants and animals, their human inhabitants, and their customs. Through his work conditions in the south-eastern part of Asia were put on record, and his travels were of the greatest help to later geographers seeking to map the world.

So far, except for the Mediterranean coastlands, little was known about Western Europe. Only when the Romans began their career of conquest was its interior systematically explored. They began with Spain, where they had first to expel the Carthaginians, and then to overcome its war-like tribes.

This work was completed by Julius Cæsar, who afterwards undertook the even more difficult task of conquering Gaul (France). This meant that his armies had not only to defeat the war-like inhabitants but also to traverse Gaul from end to end and to 'occupy' it. This he did, and later his roadmakers surveyed it. Cæsar's military despatches to the Roman Government are soldierly and keep strictly to business, without going into the picturesque details which delighted travellers such as Herodotus; but they give much information about the land and its peoples.

The natural frontier of Gaul was the Rhine, but Cæsar crossed it twice to make punitive raids upon hostile tribes in what is now Germany. Some of the later emperors sent their armies across it, hoping to master the country as far as the Elbe, but this was never accomplished. Hence, while the geography of Gaul became well known, that of the regions beyond were vague. The vast Hercynian Forest, thought except for a few clearings here and there to stretch from the Rhine to the Danube, was dark, forbidding, and swampy, harbouring great birds and bears and wild oxen and other dangerous beasts, and semi-savage tribes who were more dangerous still.

Knowing that the anti-Roman Gauls were getting support from Britain, in 55 B.C. Cæsar raided its southern coast. Although he was unprepared for the Channel tides, which wrecked many of his ships, he succeeded in landing, and later he made a second invasion. His report on the country and its people was not very accurate: he is responsible for the idea, which seems rather improbable considering our climate, that the 'Ancient Britons' wore no proper clothing but simply stained themselves blue with woad.

Though at the time Cæsar's raids accomplished little,

they prepared the way for the Romans to invade, conquer, and explore England and Wales. They never defeated the people of Scotland—indeed Hadrian had to build a wall across Northern England to keep them at bay—but about A.D. 80 the armies of General Agricola advanced to Perth, while his fleet sailed up the East Coast as far as the Orkneys, and perhaps all round Britain.

Agricola also thought of invading Ireland, and may perhaps have landed a scouting party on its shore, but he was unable to carry out his plan. Ireland traded with Roman Britain, however, and so the geographers learned something about its coast; but they knew little about its interior except that there were no snakes.

The Romans spread their own civilization throughout the lands they conquered, and so gained much information about regions hitherto unknown. This information reached the geographers, who gladly included it among their records and displayed it on their maps.

5 Geography Becomes a Science

FROM very early days maps and plans had been drawn, but these were mostly *topographical* maps, covering fairly small areas and made for special purposes: one rough plan, dated about 1300 B.C., shows the roads to the Egyptian gold-mines. The Greeks hailed their geographer, Anaximander, as the first to map the known world (about 550 B.C.).

This map was improved and given more detail, about 500 B.C., by Hecatæus, who during his studies travelled to Egypt and perhaps even further. He may have used his map as an illustration to his book, *A Description of the Earth*, the first general geography on record. As he based it mostly on information he got from seamen, it deals chiefly with the places and peoples on the Mediterranean coast.

Ideas about the world were straightforward and simple in those early days. This map shows one vast land mass, roughly circular, almost split in half by a great sea stretching from the Mediterranean through the Black Sea to the Sea of Azov, and cut into by the Gulf of Arabia on the south and by the Caspian Sea on

49

the east. Around the land was a great 'Ocean Stream', with nothing shown beyond it.

Herodotus revealed that the world was more complicated than this; he was doubtful about the Ocean Stream and believed in it only where its existence had been proved by actual voyages.

Alexandria, at the mouth of the Nile, had been built by Alexander the Great. About 283 B.C. his general Ptolemy, who had become Pharaoh of Egypt, founded the Alexandrian Museum, a university where all branches of knowledge were studied. Here the practical-minded Egyptians co-operated with the theory-loving Greeks, and together they achieved splendid results. Geography ceased to be a collection of facts and rumours, of guide-books and seamen's logs and travellers' tales. It became a science; its Greek name means, roughly, 'Describing the Earth'.

The Alexandrian scientists knew that the earth is a globe, and were ready to consider the idea that it moves, though most of them thought this unlikely. In the third century B.C. the museum's librarian, Eratosthenes, even tried to calculate its size—and came surprisingly near the truth. In drawing a world-map, he measured distances along two perpendicular lines, north-to-south and east-to-west, intersecting at the island of Rhodes. Over a century later, the astronomer Hipparchus suggested that the whole map might be covered with a grid of lines parallel to these—the origin of our latitude and longitude.

These lines were afterwards used by Strabo, who in the first century A.D. wrote another of the general geographies, descriptions of the known earth; it was intended for educated people interested in the world, and especially in its most civilized parts. Not only did he describe the different countries, but he discussed the problems of geographical science. He also gave a short history of exploration, in which he cast doubt on the value of Herodotus' enquiries and the discoveries made by Hanno and Pytheas. Not being himself a traveller, he did not realize what a surprising place the world can be.

Although large maps were sometimes posted up for public study, Strabo realized that the outlines of land and sea could not be represented correctly on a flat surface. It would take a globe to show them, and he thought that to give enough detail to be useful the globe would have to be at least ten feet across.

He may have been thinking of a globe of similar size said to have been made by Crates, royal librarian at Pergamum in Asia Minor. As all the known lands were crowded together in one quarter, the rest of the world seemed nothing but one great sea. Crates considered this unlikely; he imagined there must be three unknown countries in the other quarters: one south of Asia, another west of Europe, and another south of that. Though the thinkers of the time thought this notion fanciful, it had a great effect on later geographers, and on the history of exploration—which showed, indeed, that the idea was not so far-fetched as it seemed.

Many of the geographies were 'popularizations', meant for people who did not want to study the subject too seriously. One of these was written, in Latin, by the Roman author Pliny. He had ready very widely, and believed most of what he read, so that his *Natural History* is like a gossipy encyclopædia, full of interesting and often incredible descriptions. Yet Pliny was a serious student and a man of public spirit. He went to the assistance of the victims of the eruption of Vesuvius in A.D. 79, and was himself stifled by the volcanic gases.

The growing power of Rome brought many new discoveries for the geographers to describe and map; in the west Gaul and Britain were surveyed, and in the east other lands were explored. When Egypt was merged in the Roman Empire, its eastern trade flourished; in one year over a hundred ships might sail from the Red Sea for India or North-Eastern Africa. At first the India-bound vessels roughly followed the shore-line; however, this was not only lengthy, but also took them too near to the Arab sheikhs on the coast, who might make them pay tribute.

About the beginning of the Christian era the Greek merchant Hippalus sought a more direct route. He knew the general shape of the Arabian Sea, and he knew too that it is traversed by regular seasonal winds, the monsoons, which blow alternately north-east and south-west. At the proper season, he daringly left the Arabian coast to cross the open sea, and the monsoon brought him to the mouth of the Indus; when the wind changed he returned by a slightly different route.

Other traders, making use of what were called the
'Hippalus Winds', found an even quicker and safer
route somewhat further south to the Gulf of Cambay.

But heavy seas and sandbanks made this part of the
Indian coast dangerous; moreover, the most profitable
trading was still further south. One trader, caught
unexpectedly by a monsoon, was blown right to
Taprobane (Ceylon); he returned with an embassy to
the Roman emperor. This unexpected landfall embold-
ened some unknown merchant, about A.D. 50, to sail
and trim his sails to follow a curved course 'bulging'
slightly northwards and on his return a different route
'bulging' slightly southwards. These routes were afterwards regularly followed by the East Indiamen of
Roman times.

Some of their methods are described by the geographers. Pliny says that travellers should set out down the
Red Sea when the Dog Star (Sirius) rises just before
the sun; they should reach the open sea in about thirty
days, and if 'Hippalus Winds' were blowing strongly
they should reach South India about forty days later.

A merchant's handbook dated about A.D. 60 gives
details about the peoples and trading possibilities of
part of the Indian coast, together with such sailing
directions as a warning that in the Strait of Babel-
mandeb the current and winds are violent. The pilot
may know when he is approaching the Indian coast
not only because the colour of the water changes, but
also because of the many sea-snakes, 'coloured bright
green and gold'; near the Gulf of Cutch, where

shallows and shifting sandbanks, rip-tides and over-falls, make the approach difficult, the sea-snakes are much larger, and their colour is black. In the Gulf of Cambay, also very dangerous, the king organized a pilot-service for ships that had to be towed upriver to his city.

Commerce with India prospered, and the Greek traders went exploring inland and reached several of its towns. They visited Ceylon and the Maldive Islands, and even pushed up the east coast of India as far as the Ganges delta. The Bay of Bengal is also traversed by monsoons; though these are not so regular as those in the Arabian Sea, they are fairly reliable, and are a great help to navigation.

The first to make use of them was an explorer called Alexander, who began by traversing the Bay in a series of 'hops' from the Indian coast north of Ceylon to a town just south of the 20th parallel of latitude, then due east to the coast of Burma, then almost south to Cape Negrais, and then on to Malaya. Other traders, much as in the Arabian Sea, found later that the monsoons could take them across much more directly; they sailed from the north of Ceylon, with a slight northern 'bulge', to Malaya, returning by a different route with a slight southern 'bulge' from either Malaya or Sumatra.

Alexander had meantime pushed on beyond Malaya, crossed the Gulf of Siam, and travelled up the coast to the Gulf of Tong-King. Later explorers ventured even further to the coast of China itself; the outward and return journey from Egypt needed supplies for three years.

All the information gained from these distant parts, and elsewhere, had to be included in the geographies and maps. This was most efficiently done about A.D. 150 by Ptolemy. He was an astronomer and a mathematician, and his *Geography* is not so much a description of the earth as a textbook on scientific map-making. What he called 'chatter about the ways of peoples' did not interest him; he was seeking to chart the earth. He explains the lines of latitude and longitude, and the method of combining them with the outlines of land and sea. Though positions ought really to be fixed by observations of the sun and stars, this, he admits, was seldom possible, and the geographer would have to rely on travellers' records, allowance being made for their over-statements and errors.

Using such information, Ptolemy listed about eight thousand places—countries, islands, rivers, mountains, cities, the homes of tribes—and estimated the latitude and longitude of each. From these figures maps could be drawn of any region, or even of the whole earth.

Unfortunately, even the best information he could get was not very accurate, and he did not realize how greatly travellers are apt to over-estimate the distances they cover. So maps based on his figures were bound to be distorted, and copyists' errors could distort them still more (as printing had not been invented, all copies had to be made laboriously by hand, and tired copyists easily make mistakes). A map of Britain based on his figures shows Scotland leaning perpendicularly over the east coast of England.

Ptolemy over-estimated the east-to-west breadth of Asia, and under-estimated the size of the earth. So he 'overstretched' his great landmass, making it extend half-way round the globe. For some reason he also thought that the Indian Ocean was a huge inland sea, closed in on the south by another great landmass joining Africa to China.

Many centuries later these errors had surprising effects on geography and exploration. In spite of them, however, Ptolemy's work gave the greatest help to navigators of his own time. But soon the Roman Empire was overrun by raiders whose existence Ptolemy had not suspected. Civilization was almost destroyed, and, in the Dark Ages that followed, people were fully occupied with local affairs; all that was known of distant lands consisted of vague legends and preposterous horror-stories of incredible peoples and beasts.

6 Missionaries, Monks and Pilgrims

OBEDIENT to Christ's command to go into the world and preach His gospel to every creature, some of His followers travelled far. Even in civilized regions they had to face great perils: when St. Paul was shipwrecked off Malta, the seamen tried to abandon ship, leaving the hapless passengers to their fate.

Ancient tradition has it that some of the Apostles travelled further afield; St. James to Spain, St. Andrew to Russia, St. Bartholomew to Armenia, and St. Thomas to Mesopotamia and possibly to India. These were some of the first Christian missionaries, and soon others followed them, so that in later centuries they are heard of in the most remote and unexpected places. Though not actually aiming at discovery, the missionaries brought knowledge of distant regions back to the civilized lands.

The motives of other travellers were different but equally religious: not to spread the Gospel but to visit the sites whence it came: these pilgrims, too, brought information about foreign parts. Soon there were so many of them that routes were worked out, and guide-books written. These give the geographers an idea of the world in the early-Christian era.

One of these first guide-books, *An Itinerary from Bordeaux to Jerusalem*, by way of Constantinople (formerly called Byzantium and now renamed Istanbul), covers a distance of nearly two thousand four hundred miles; it mentions about three hundred post-houses where fresh horses could be obtained, and 170 places on the route, and in describing the Holy Land it 'identifies' sites of religious interest, including the burial places of Abraham and his family and the battle-field where David slew Goliath.

St. Helena was perhaps the most famous of these early pilgrims, for when in A.D. 326 she made the long and difficult journey to Jerusalem, she was reputed to have discovered the 'true Cross' on which Christ had been crucified. As she was the mother of the Byzantine emperor Constantine, knowledge of her achievement spread far and wide and did much to encourage pilgrimage.

One fourth-century pilgrim, Etheria of Aquitaine, sent home an account of her travels among the biblical sites in the Near East. Among other achievements she climbed Mount Sinai and enjoyed the wide view from its summit, and after visiting Jerusalem she went on to the borders of Persia. During her four-year pilgrimage, she travelled 2000 miles, and planned to go even further into Asia.

Religious pilgrimages did not begin with Christianity; nor were they limited to Christendom. A very long and very arduous pilgrimage was made in the seventh century by a monk of the Buddhist religion. This religion, which spread across Asia, was founded in the sixth century B.C. by Gautama Buddha, an Indian prince who gave up his throne to devote his life to the quest for truth.

In A.D. 629 the Chinese monk Hiuen-Tsiang, anxious to learn more about Buddhist teachings and to get copies of its sacred books, visited the land whence his religion came. It was forbidden to leave China, and so he had to escape by night, evading hot pursuit.

After crossing a river on an improvised brushwood bridge, the monk had to follow the tracks across the vast Gobi Desert by looking for the bones of men and camels who had died by the wayside.

For five days he was completely lost, until his horse scented water. When at last he reached the mountains he nearly froze to death.

Though the chieftains honoured him as a holy man, entertained him at banquets, and listened respectfully to his teachings, this was actually a disadvantage, for they refused to part with him, and relented only when he threatened to refuse all food.

Hiuen-Tsiang pushed on by Samarkand and through the Khyber Pass into Kashmir. There he found a learned Buddhist monk, with whom he stayed two years. The next fourteen years were spent in traversing India from Nepal to Ceylon, visiting monasteries and other centres of learning, studying and teaching and collecting religious books. The people interested him greatly, with their ways of life so different from his own.

In A.D. 643 he went back up the Khyber Pass, through the storm-swept Pamir Valley, then across the desert by a different route from that of his outward journey, past a bleak lake, the Lob Nor. In spite of further perils and hardships, attacks by robbers, and the loss of much valuable equipment when the elephant which carried it fell into a ravine, he arrived home safely.

He had left China almost like a refugee. He returned in triumph, with a score of horses carrying hundreds of books, and images and relics of Buddha. The emperor who had denied him permission to leave now welcomed him, treated him as a friend, and offered him a position at court. But Hiuen-Tsiang declined such honours, and spent the rest of his life translating into Chinese the Buddhist manuscripts which he had gained. Valuable though these are to students of religion, geographers are more interested in the conditions in Asia described in the record of his travels which the emperor induced him to write.

Many of the more devout Christians 'forsook the world', and became monks or nuns, and when the Roman Empire fell before the barbarian attacks they did much to preserve and then to restore civilization and culture. Others spread it even beyond the boundaries of the Empire.

About the beginning of the fifth century a boy of sixteen was kidnapped by pirates from his home on the shores of the Severn and sold as a slave in Ireland. This cruel treatment did not embitter him but deepened his faith, and after he escaped his one desire was to return to spread the Gospel among the people who had ill-used him. So well did he succeed that he is now honoured as St. Patrick, Patron Saint of Ireland.

After being trained as a priest and visiting Rome in A.D. 432, he began his life's work as a missionary, boldly facing the High King in his court at Tara and insisting on his right to preach. He travelled throughout the length and breadth of Ireland, preaching, converting, founding churches and monasteries and nunneries. Through his work, the country became a great centre of Christianity and civilization, and sent missionaries to other lands.

One of the greatest of these was St. Columba, who, in A.D. 563, set off with twelve followers across the sea to Iona, a Scottish islet not far from Oban. Here the monastery he founded became a centre for the conversion of Scotland and the North of England. St. Columba not only penetrated the Highlands, but even sailed as far as the Orkneys, and many of his followers also made arduous and perilous journeys.

The Irish missionaries who set out westwards had some very remarkable experiences. Cormac, a follower of St. Columba, driven north by a gale for fourteen days, reached a land where there were 'dreadful stinging creatures'—possibly the vicious Greenland mosquitoes.

The legends told about St. Brendan (or Brandon) are almost as strange as those described in the *Odyssey*,

and attempts have similarly been made to ascertain
the facts upon which they are based. St. Brendan made
three long voyages in quest of the 'Island of Saints',
travelling in a large *curragh*, a very light boat made of
a thin wicker framework covered with ox-hides; and
among his supplies was the butter needed to keep the
hides greased.

When they were too tired to row, St. Brendan told
his companions to ship their oars, even the steering-oar,
and to let the wind take them where it would: God
would be their 'pilot and steersman'. The wind took
them, the legends say, to a number of remarkable
islands. One was the 'island of sheep, where it is always
summer'; this may have been Madeira. Another was
covered with singing birds, and another was volcanic.
One, on which they landed and kindled a fire, began to
quiver beneath them, and they had to hasten back
into their boat—it was really the back of a whale!
They sailed into a sea which seemed to be 'clogged',
which sounds rather like the 'sea-lung' mentioned by
Pytheas, and they saw a column, so high that it seemed
to pierce the clouds, made of the clearest crystal and
as hard as rock: this description of an iceberg, with
some other details, shows that they had actually
reached the Arctic.

For a long time 'St. Brendan's Isle', the Island of
the Blessed, figured a little vaguely on the Atlantic
charts, its position changing as knowledge of the seas
increased, and it played an important part in the
history of discovery. Only in the eighteenth century

was it finally dropped, and it is now thought to have been a mirage—an appearance of distant lands caused by the air's refraction and said to arouse a strange sense of 'yearning'.

In the ninth century a monk called Dicuil, who was also a geographer, tried to describe the islands in the far north; his description of a group where hermits had once lived refers to the Faroes. Even more interesting is his statement that some monks had lived on Thule; this shows that a monastery once existed in Iceland. The adventurous monks who reached that distant country may have found their way across the sea by following the annual migration of geese and other birds from Britain to the summer breeding-grounds in Ireland and Iceland. Aided by a favourable wind, rowing during the calms, and getting their direction from the 'skeins' of birds which flew above them, the monks might have found their way there fairly easily.

7 The Arabs

IN THE seventh century Mohammed founded the Moslem religion, and his Arab followers set out to spread it by force. Their empire extended from Turkestan and the borders of India along the northern coast of Africa to Spain; only after severe fighting was it kept out of France. It even threatened the Byzantine Empire. This was the eastern part of what had been the Roman Empire, and its capital was Constantinople.

These conquests involved much exploration. The new empire was linked by a flourishing trade, and pious Moslems were expected to make a pilgrimage to Mohammed's birthplace at Mecca. Even their daily prayers demanded a knowledge of latitude and longitude. Because local time, as shown by the sun, varies from place to place, sundials had to be specially made to suit local conditions; and because the worshipper had to face Mecca, he had to know the exact direction in which the 'Holy City' lay.

Studying geography for such reasons, the Arabs were greatly helped by the writings of Ptolemy and the other great scientists of old, and they were also in contact with the thinkers of Europe, India, and China. They worked out the latitude and longitude of many regions so accurately as to show that even the great Ptolemy had seriously over-estimated the length of the Mediterranean.

The 'father of Arab geography' was Jakoubi, who not merely consulted other travellers from east and west, but was himself an explorer. His *Book of Countries*, dated about 900, gave the names of many places, their distances apart and descriptions of their chief features and of their inhabitants. It was free from one of the faults to which Arab writers were prone, to mingle fable with fact.

Several Arab travellers made journeys to China. Among other interesting facts, they explained how tea was made and said it was very good for the health; they praised the excellence of the ware which we still call 'china', as clear and fine as glass, and the high standard of Chinese education. One such journey extended from Armenia to the Volga, north of the Caspian, across the Urals to the Altai Mountains in Mongolia, and back by way of Bokhara to Iraq.

c

Some of the Arab expeditions are described more vaguely, and we cannot be certain how far they extended. One is said to have found the source of the Nile, always something of a mystery, in an African lake; and to have reached the 'Mountains of the Moon' between Lakes Edward and Albert. One voyage, made first to the 'Sea of Darkness', the Northern Atlantic, and then southward, mentions an island far out in the ocean inhabited by tall 'red' men with smooth hair. Although this sounds rather like the discovery of America, it is thought to refer to Madeira, but even so it was the first voyage of discovery into the Atlantic since Hanno had coasted North-West Africa and Pytheas had heard of Thule.

One Arab geographer, Alburini, who accompanied a Moslem army which invaded India about 1027, was able from his own experience to write a very useful description of that country. He also wrote a book on the methods which different peoples use for reckoning time, and another on the geography of Central Asia, including Turkestan, Nepal, and Tibet.

As civilization revived in Western Europe, the Christians became indignant that Palestine, the birthplace of their religion, should be ruled by the Moslems, and that pilgrimages to Jerusalem should be interfered with. From the end of the eleventh century onwards they launched a series of Crusades, whose object was to free the Holy Places from domination by the infidels. They failed; but the attempt brought them into contact not only with the Byzantine Empire, but also with the Arab civilization, which was far more advanced scientifically than their own.

They learned much from both, and many a Christian prince was glad to have a Mohammedan wise man as an adviser at his court. One, employed by King Roger of Sicily, was Edrisi: born in Spain, he had travelled widely in Europe, where he reached the English Channel, and in Asia Minor. He also gained much information from seamen and merchants, and his book *The Rogerian Treatise*, written about 1170, describes the geography of Europe in more detail than the earlier Arab writers. Though the maps he himself drew are not very accurate, the knowledge he brought to Sicily enabled its map-makers to produce excellent charts.

Some of the adventures related by *Sindbad the Sailor* are based on actual experience, helped out by the story-teller's imagination; as with the *Odyssey* and St. Brendan, attempts have been made to find what these experiences were.

Sindbad's first voyage is thought to have taken him to Borneo. The description of an immense fish which could be scared away by knocking pieces of wood together suggests that the narrator had heard about the encounter of Nearchus with the whales. That of an owl-faced fish may refer to the parrot wrasse, a tropical fish with beak-like jaws. The drums beaten on a small island by 'evil spirits' may simply be the sound of waves echoing in a cave.

The huge beast 'called rhinoceros' with one great

horn in the centre of its forehead was seen by Sindbad on an island which might be Sumatra or Java. The valley full of jewels but abounding in venomous snakes sounds like one of the 'horror stories' by which the diamond merchants tried to discourage search for the mines.

The island inhabited by 'hairy folk like apes' might be Borneo, and the huge serpent Sindbad mentions on another island might possibly be the twelve-foot monitor (giant lizard) of Komodo. The 'Old Man of the Sea' said to have enslaved him may be an idea suggested by the sight of the orang-utan, with its flexible legs.

The description of the Roc, a bird so immense that it could fly away with an elephant, is probably based on a voyage to Madagascar. Here a bird, the Aepyornis, though now extinct, may have survived until 'Sindbad's' time: it was over seven feet high, and its eggs, which the natives used as buckets, would hold two and a half gallons and were about three feet round. Add to this the frond of a Magadascan palm tree which looks rather like a gigantic feather, and it is easy how the idea of the Roc may have begun. True, Aepyornis was actually a wingless bird, but the narrator may not have known this, and even if he did, he could hardly be expected to spoil a good story for the sake of a detail like that!

8 Vikings by Land and Sea

LARGELY through the good work of the monasteries, civilization revived in Europe. Then again it was threatened, by the attacks of fierce sea-raiders, the Vikings (Vik-ings, 'Men of the fjords') from Scandinavia. 'From the fury of the Norsemen, Good Lord deliver us', was the prayer which went up in the churches of North-East England.

To the Vikings themselves, however, these raids were real explorations of unknown lands. At first they came only to loot and destroy, but soon they realized that they would do far better to occupy and colonize these foreign shores. They needed colonies, too, for their own lands were getting overcrowded, and they had either to emigrate or to starve. So their young men set out adventurously in their dragon-headed galleys, rowed not unwillingly by slaves but enthusiastically by warriors, and they ranged ever further afield.

They might well have conquered all England had not Alfred the Great defeated them, and even then he had to allow them to retain the eastern part of England, called the Dane-law—but in return Alfred made them accept Christianity. Under their leader Rolf the Ganger they also conquered part of Northern France;

and here these Normans (North-men) not only accepted Christianity but dropped their own language and learned to speak French. In both countries they inter-mingled with the original inhabitants and adopted their civilization.

Though not himself an explorer, Alfred was well aware of the value of discovery and the need for know-ledge of foreign lands. He translated and revised a geographical book written in Latin some centuries before by a Spanish priest, Orosius, and in bringing it up to date he was willing to learn even from his for-mer enemies the Norsemen. He was greatly interested when Othere, a Norwegian sea-captain, told him of a hazardous journey he had made into the far north.

Othere lived 'the farthest north of any Northman', at Halgoland, in Norway, near the Lofoten Islands; beyond, the land was almost uninhabited except for some hunters and fishers whom he called 'Fynnes' but who were really Laplanders. He had the true ex-plorer's spirit, for about 880 he sailed north simply to see how far the land went. Always keeping the coast to starboard, he sailed almost north-east for six days, three days more than the walrus-hunters usually ventured. Then the run of the coast changed, and he turned east-south-east for another four days; then it changed again, and he had to wait for a north wind. So, having rounded the North Cape, he sailed into the White Sea, and as evidence of his adventurous journey he gave the king a walrus-tooth.

    •   •   •   •   •

Other Northmen, mostly from Sweden, sailed not across the sea but up the rivers of Europe. In the ninth century they cruised into the Gulf of Riga and up the Dwina; they then made a portage, carrying their boats across country to a southward-flowing river which joined the Dnieper; having captured Kiev they journeyed downstream to the Black Sea. Thence, early in the tenth century, they turned northwards into the Sea of Azov and sailed up the rivers which flow into it; another portage brought them to the Volga, which took them into the Caspian Sea. Both the Black Sea and the Caspian served them as bases from which to raid the neighbouring lands.

To the astonished Eastern peoples, the coming of these Varangians, as they called themselves (from a Scandinavian word meaning 'confederates'), was as horrifying as that of the Vikings had been to the English.

The Varangians had heard, rather vaguely, that somewhere in Southern Europe was a fine, wealthy city, which they called Micklegarth ('great city'). Here, on the shore of the Black Sea, they found it. So their vessels, small but very numerous, concentrated to threaten Constantinople, capital of the Byzantine Empire.

The Emperor realized not only the danger of having such warriors as his enemies, but also the value of having them as friends. Instead of fighting them, he enlisted them, and they became his bodyguard, the Imperial Varangians. Soon reinforcements joined

them, for their fame spread across Europe, and the
Norman Conquest sent exiled English and Danes to
seek refuge in their ranks.

Further north, the Viking raiders had been even
more successful. In 862 their leader Rurik, probably a
Dane, captured and became the ruler of Novgorod.
His successor Duke Olav, who had taken Kiev, founded
a state which has grown to form modern Russia.

Meantime the Vikings had also been 'island hopping'
across the Atlantic, conquering the northern part of
Ireland and cruising down the Irish Sea. They colonized the Orkneys and the Shetlands, and later the
Faroe Islands. About 880 a 'great Viking', Naddodd,
seeking to return from Norway to his home in the
Faroes, was driven westwards by the wind into the seas
beyond. There he found a great land which seemed to
be uninhabited; because of its wintry appearance he
called it Snowland. Then Garda, a Swede, similarly
driven off-course while making for Scotland, cruised
round this newly-discovered country and so proved
that it was an island. So pleasant did he find it that
later he returned to make his home there.

Another 'great Viking', Floki, went, by way of the
Shetlands, to search for what was called 'Garda's
Holme' (island). He took three ravens with him, and
released them one by one: the first flew back eastward;
the second simply returned to the ship; but the third
soared onwards, showing that there was land somewhere ahead. At last he sighted this and coasted it

westward to Snaefelness; from the summit of a mountain he saw a glacier, and so he called the country Iceland.

Floki and his men were not the first to reach Iceland, for in a few places they found what they called 'Papar', monks and priests, as well as Irish emigrants. But they were the first to colonize and develop it; this especially attracted seekers of adventure, unruly people who could not get on with their neighbours, and a sprinkling of outlaws.

One outlaw, Eric the Red, was too unruly even for Iceland, and was banished again. While seeking for some distant islands called after their discoverer 'Gunbjorn's Skerries', he reached an uninhabited country. It was so well wooded and had such rich meadows that he called it Greenland, and soon this newly-founded country was being colonized. It was uninhabited, but there were the remains of huts; the explorers uneasily feared that these had been built by 'trolls' (ogres) and shunned them as uncanny.

A trader, Bjarni Herjulfason, hearing that his father had gone to Greenland, decided to follow him, although he knew this was rash, for neither he nor his crew had ever been in those waters. The winds were contrary, and the sky hidden by fog, and for several days they sailed at random; then, after the sky had cleared, they found themselves near a coast. But this, Bjarni realized, could not be Greenland, for the nights were too long and its woods were free from snow. Taking advantage of a favourable wind, he returned to Greenland, where his adventure aroused much excitement.

About A.D. 1000 Leif Ericsson decided to investigate this unknown country. Cruising westward with thirty-five companions, he reached a barren shore, covered with scree and backed by snow-clad mountains; he called it Helluland ('Flatstone Country'). Turning southwards, he found a region of swamp forest, which he called Markland ('Bush Country'), and beyond this was a grassy tract, 'where the dew tasted sweet'. Reaching a river-mouth, he sailed upstream to a lake, where he built huts to form a centre from which to explore the country; he found this so pleasant, and so rich in grapes, that he called it Vineland the Good. Taking on board a cargo of grapes and timber, he returned to spread news of this discovery in Greenland.

Soon settlers were going out to colonize Vineland. They reached it without much trouble, but soon they found it was not uninhabited: they met some strange-looking natives, whom they called Skraelings. None-theless several colonies were established: that headed by Karlsefne included two shiploads of emigrants, one hundred and fifty men and several women, with their cattle, sheep, ponies, dogs, and poultry. The colonists made several journeys of exploration across country and upstream, and erected forts protected by wooden stockades.

The colonies in Vineland lasted for several centuries. But they were too far from the homeland to get proper support, and the hostile Skraelings got increasingly troublesome. At last they had to be abandoned, and now their situations are unknown. It is not even certain what regions the Viking explorers reached, nor who their enemies were. Helluland may have been in Labrador or Newfoundland, Markland in Nova Scotia, and Vineland in New England; the Skraelings may have been Eskimos or Red Indians, or both—and they were probably the 'trolls' whose ruined huts had been found in Greenland.

So the Viking attempt to colonize America failed, but its memory lived on in the Sagas, the Scandinavian epic poems. It may have spread southwards as a vague rumour, and so encouraged the later adventurers who hoped to find habitable countries across the Atlantic.

9 Eastward across the Land

THE Christians and Mohammedans were still fighting each other, and still learning from one another, when, in the thirteenth century, both alike were threatened by a new enemy. A great leader, Genghis Khan, united the Mongols, the nomadic horsemen of Central Asia, and led them to the conquest of China. After his death his son Ogdai Khan led them westwards, conquering much of Asia and the eastern part of Europe. Their use of gunpowder and their fighting spirit made them almost irresistible; their westward advance ceased not because they had been defeated in battle, but partly because the woods of Central Europe hindered them, and partly because of disputes among their rulers after the death of Ogdai Khan.

76

Though naturally alarmed at the irruption of the Mongols, the Christians of Europe hoped to turn it to good account by converting the invaders and making an alliance with them against their older enemies, the Moslem Turks. They sent missionaries to visit the Mongol headquarters at Karakorum, and these missionaries made useful explorations of the unknown regions which they had to traverse.

The first was a Franciscan monk, John de Plano Carpini, whom the Pope sent in 1245 with a message to the Mongol ruler, the Great Khan. Accompanied by two other monks and led by a guide, Carpini travelled through Bohemia and then, by way of Cracow and Kiev, down the Dnieper and across the Volga. Beyond lay unknown country, the most difficult part of their journey; not knowing whether it would be 'for life or death', they set out, as Carpini said, 'most tearfully'—but neither their tears nor their fears kept them from setting out.

Their journey was hard and perilous: though they used Tartar horses, the only ones that could find grass under the snow in lands where there was neither hay nor straw, they became so thin that none of them could ride, and Carpini, who was ill, had to travel in a cart. Yet they journeyed on, north of the Caspian and Aral Seas, past the Tian Shan Mountains, and through the Altai Mountains to the Tartar camp near Karakorum, where they witnessed the splendour as a new Great Khan was enthroned.

Though the new khan received them politely, they

could not convert him, and he sent them back with a
message to the Pope. In spite of even worse hardships
on the return journey, they succeeded in delivering it.

Carpini's *Book of the Tartars* gives much interesting
information. He describes the soil round Karakorum as
'everywhere sandy and barren'; the weather, very in-
temperate, with thunderstorms mingled with snow-
storms, cold bleak tempests so fierce that a man could
not keep on his horse, little rain but much hail, and
sudden changes from great heat to great cold. He was
much interested in the nomads' tents, each with a
window near the top to let the light in and the smoke
out, and so constructed of felt and wicker and staves
that they could be very easily struck and pitched: and
he says that while the Tartars possessed many other
cattle, they thought they had more horses and mares
than the rest of the world. One of the things which
most impressed the three friars was the contrast
between the simple lives of the tribesmen and the
splendour at the court of the Great Khan.

The next envoy to the Mongols, William of Rubruck,
was sent in 1252, not by the Pope but by Louis IX
of France, then in Palestine leading a crusade. Accompanied by two other Franciscan friars, William sailed
to Constantinople and across the Black Sea to the
Crimea; the rest of their journey was made not on
horseback but by cart, and involved many hardships.

At last they reached the camp of a Mongol lord on
the Volga; he angrily refused to be converted, and sent
them on to Karakorum by much the same route as

that which had been followed by Carpini. Mangu Khan, the Tartar ruler, received them kindly, but he too refused to become a Christian—indeed his chief interest in the envoys seemed to be to learn what were his chances of conquering France. Though wearied and enfeebled, and though William, who as a friar had to walk barefoot, was suffering from frost-bite, they at last returned to Asia Minor.

Like Carpini, William wrote an account of his travels, and this likewise gives much interesting information about the Mongols and their country. It was useful, too, to the European geographers of the time, for William explains carefully that the Caspian Sea was not, as some of them seem to have thought, 'a bay or gulf coming forth of the ocean . . . but is invironed in on all sides by land'.

One effect of the Mongol conquests had been to open up Asia for trade, and soon two Venetian merchants, Nicolò and Maffeo Polo, were taking advantage of this. They travelled across the Black Sea to Serai near the Volga, where they stayed some time trading. Then, finding that to return home was impossible because of a war, they decided to push on to Bokhara, and there a Tartar nobleman invited them to travel to the court of the Great Khan, Kublai, which had now been moved to Peking, in China.

Kublai Khan was much interested in them, for they were the first Europeans he had seen. They stayed at his court for some time; and when at last they returned to

Venice after fifteen years' absence, they brought his request for a hundred thinkers to teach the Law of Christ.

Unfortunately, only two friars were found willing to make the journey, but when in 1271 the Polo brothers returned to Peking they also took with them Nicolò's son, Marco, then seventeen years old. They had meant to travel by sea, but, thinking that the vessels offered them were unseaworthy, they went overland instead, across the Pamira to Kashgar and then across the Gobi Desert. In spite of a year's delay caused by Marco's illness, they arrived in 1275 at Peking.

Kublai Khan was glad to welcome his old friends the elder Polos, and especially to welcome young Marco, who was plainly intelligent, and so keen he had already mastered the Tartar language. He not only gave him a position at court, but also employed him on several official missions, and even appointed him governor of a Chinese city, Yang-chow. Marco carried out these tasks efficiently, and for sixteen years he and his two relatives lived happily in China, profiting by the opportunities of trade.

At last they grew homesick, and they feared, too, that after Kublai's death the new khan might not favour them and that their rivals would make trouble. Kublai did not wish to part with them, but at last he allowed them to escort a Chinese princess westwards by sea to marry his brother, the Persian king.

They were so delayed by bad weather and other hindrances that the journey took two years, and by the time they arrived the king was dead. So instead the princess married his son; and then the Polos, their duty performed, went home to Venice.

They had been away twenty-four years, and when they returned, weary and travel-stained and ragged, few of the Venetians recognized them, and nobody knew what to make of them. The story goes that they gave a great feast to their friends, afterwards sending for the battered garments in which they had travelled. While everybody was staring amazed, they ripped open the seams, and out poured a multitude of 'rubies, sapphires, carbuncles, emeralds, and diamonds', the proceeds of their trade in the Far East.

After this, naturally, there was no question about their being welcomed, but still the people were rather amused by Marco's endless descriptions of rich cities and well-populated countries at the ends of the earth, of millions of ducats and millions of people. *Il Milione* became his nickname, 'the million man'.

In those days Italy was disunited, and its small city-states were often at war. In a battle between Venice and Genoa *Il Milione* was taken prisoner, and he whiled away his dreary captivity by describing his adventures to a friend, Rusticiano. That friend afterwards published them, and *The Travels of Marco Polo* became one of the world's great books. Full of exciting detail and very interesting to read, it stirred the imaginations of thinking people and made them anxious to visit those distant lands and to see for themselves the wonders described by Marco, to trade with those foreign peoples, and to come home, like the three Polos, with their garments full to bursting with jewels.

Marco Polo was one of the world's greatest explorers. Not only did he accomplish amazing journeys in spite of illness and hardship, but he also carefully observed the lands he traversed and the peoples he met; and though he did not himself publish a record of his experiences, he described them so vividly that his friend Rusticiano was able to give them to the world.

Before crossing the great Gobi Desert, he explains, travellers need a week's rest to prepare for the ordeal, and they have to take a month's supply of food for man and beast. For the desert consists of hills and valleys of sand, where nothing can be found to eat. There are about twenty-eight springs, a day's journey apart, which provide fresh water for a caravan of not more than a hundred people; and there are also four springs of brackish water. The animals must have bells tied to their necks to prevent their going astray, and the travellers must keep together, not only to avoid getting lost, but lest they should be lured away by the evil spirits supposed to haunt the desert. At sleeping-time a signal is put up to show the direction of the next march—'so it is that the Desert is crossed'.

Such hardships were well rewarded, for beyond the Desert was Cambulac (Peking). This was the capital city of the 'Lord of Lords, named Kublai', who was 'of middle height, with an attractive fresh complexion, fair hair and dark eyes'. The city was walled and built four-square, its main streets so wide and straight that its twelve gates, each guarded by a thousand men, were in sight of one another. It contained many splendid houses and palaces, and near its centre was a larger palace with a steeple; after its great bell had rung three times at night, nobody was allowed to leave the city till next day.

Highways led from Cambulac to the provinces, and at every twenty miles was a post-house where the khan's messengers could get fresh horses: at some, as many as four hundred horses were kept ready for use, and to maintain them all over three hundred thousand horses were needed. Even regions where there was no road or habitation had post-houses, but here they were further apart.

Larger than Cambulac was the 'City of Heaven', Hang-chow, the capital of Manji (South China), which Marco calls the largest and finest city in the world. It was about thirty-five miles round, and in it were twelve thousand stone bridges, mostly high enough for a ship to pass under them, for the city, like Venice, was built on and surrounded by water. It also held a large lake, about ten miles round, and several thousand baths, in some of which a hundred people could bathe at once. Marco was impressed with the delight that the Chinese took in bathing and their high standards of cleanliness.

He stressed the wealth of the Hang-chow merchants and their ladies, who did nothing with their own hands but were waited on as though they were kings and queens. There were twelve trade guilds in the city, each with twelve thousand workshops employing not less than ten workmen, and here again Marco was impressed with their high standards of honesty. Silk, he noticed, was so plentiful that most of the people always wore it.

He was equally impressed with the great rivers of China, some of them miles wide and crowded with shipping; in one smallish town, indeed, there might be fifteen thousand vessels at once. The seaports, too, carried on a flourishing trade in costly spices and precious stones.

Marco also saw a very different kind of stone, a 'black stone' hewn out from the mountains and used as fuel, as it was cheaper and burned better than firewood. (Coal was then almost unknown in Europe.)

Although he did not himself visit it, he describes an island, Cipangu, some distance from the Chinese coast. Its people were fair-skinned, civilized and gentle in their manners, and so wealthy that the king paved his palace with gold. This was the first time the geographers of Europe had heard of Japan.

Polo also mentions Tibet and the East Indies, and on his journey home he visited Java, very rich in spices, and Sumatra. Here he saw what he called 'a unicorn'— a rhinoceros.

Several other explorers afterwards journeyed from Europe to distant parts of Asia. Some were traders, like the Polo brothers; others were missionaries, anxious to take Christianity to those distant lands and also interested in their marvels. In the fourteenth century Friar Odoric travelled widely in the Far East, and recorded some facts about the Chinese which Marco Polo had not mentioned. He explains that among them it was a mark of gentility, showing that a personage had never done any manual work, to let the finger-nails grow long; and that the greatest beauty among the ladies was tiny feet, so that the feet of baby girls were so tightly bandaged that they could never grow.

Odoric also visited a country which Marco Polo only mentions. Though perhaps not the first European to reach Tibet, he was the first to describe it. Polo had thought of it as almost an uninhabited wilderness, but Odoric says it was well supplied with bread and wine; though the people lived in tents of black felt, he says that its capital, Lhasa, was well built and well paved, and that within its walls no blood must be shed, either of man or beast.

A German, Hans Schiltberger, became an explorer against his will, for in 1396 he was taken prisoner by the Turks. After being kept captive for some time in Samarkand, he went deeper into Siberia than any previous traveller, into the province of Tobolsk and Tomsk. Among other interesting facts, he mentions the use of sledge-dogs.

Another fourteenth-century explorer, the Arab Ibn Battuta, travelled even more widely than Marco Polo. He journeyed through Arabia, Persia, and the Yemen, and across Asia Minor into Russia, perhaps as far as

Siberia, and by both land and sea to China; he also visited the Maldive Islands, which he is the first explorer to describe.

Realizing that he had seen most of the Moslem countries, he decided to visit the others, so from his home in Tangier he went southwards into Africa. Crossing the Atlas Mountains and the Sahara, he reached what he thought was the Nile: it was really the Niger. Travelling downstream from Timbuktu in a dug-out canoe, he afterwards returned to Tangier by a different route. Though he was less interested in places than in people, he had done what he had set out to do, by describing life in the Moslem world and elsewhere.

In the same century appeared a remarkable book, the *Travels* of Sir John Mandeville. Full of astonishing statements, and in some editions startlingly illustrated, it describes such marvels as giants thirty feet high, dancing pygmies, the pillar of salt into which Lot's wife was transformed, and the barn which Joseph constructed to enable Pharaoh to store his grain ready for the Seven Years' Famine (the Pyramids).

Far from being an explorer, 'Sir John'—if that indeed were his real name—may never have travelled in his life. Though where his *Travels* are not cribbed from other writers they are sheer romancing, they are very amusing. By making their readers want to see such wonders for themselves they may even have encouraged exploration.

Among the marvels described not only by Mandeville but also in more serious travel-books was one especially inspiring to the Christians of Europe. Somewhere vaguely in the heart of heathen Asia, it was said, was a great Christian country ruled by a king of incredible wealth and power, Prester John. Nobody ever succeeded in finding this kingdom, but several attempts have been made to account for the rumours about it.

One suggestion is that in days when people's idea of geography were hazy, the Christian kingdom may have been not in Asia but in Africa: Ethiopia (Abyssinia), whose monarch claims descent from King Solomon. Another is that the story refers to a fairly powerful but short-lived Christian state which for a short time flourished in North China during the twelfth century. Another is that it refers to Tibet, where the impressive Buddhist ceremonies may have seemed, to bewildered travellers who did not understand the language, like some outlandish form of Christian worship.

10 Sea-route to the East

LAND travel to the Far East, difficult and dangerous at best, became even more hazardous when the Ottoman Turks began a career of conquest which led to their capturing Constantinople and mastering the Balkan Peninsula. Sea travel was easier once the Indian Ocean was reached, but to reach it merchandise had to be shipped down the Mediterranean, transported across the Isthmus of Suez, and then re-shipped down the stormy Red Sea. It might be interfered with by the Turks, and the Eastern trade was largely controlled by the city-states of Italy, who charged very heavily for their services. Plainly some more convenient route was needed, and in the fifteenth century systematic attempts were made to discover it, especially as the Spice Islands (the Moluccas) were attracting many trading-vessels.

The Moors of the Iberian Peninsula had been driven into the southern mountains, and the greater part of the land was now ruled by Christians. Situated on the western coast, Portugal was in an especially favourable position for sea-travel, and such travel was greatly developed by one of its princes.

Prince Henry of Portugal, born in 1394 and descended on his mother's side from the English royal family, was a man both of knowledge and of action. He was keenly interested in mathematics and geography, and he not only organized the fleet which captured the Moroccan city of Ceuta, but led the landing-party to its attack. The victory left him even more curious than before about the remote parts of the earth, and soon he began organizing systematic attempts to explore them.

As a prince he was anxious to increase his country's power and prosperity. As a Christian he was anxious to overcome the widespread Moslem power and to make an alliance with Prester John, whose kingdom might be somewhere in Africa. And as a thinker he was anxious to learn more about the unknown parts of the earth.

There was much to favour him. The Turkish conquest of the Balkans had driven a number of monks westwards into exile; they brought with them copies of the ancient Greek writings—including the works of Ptolemy. The compass had been invented and improved, and other instruments had been devised for taking a ship's bearings at sea. Mapping had advanced greatly: instead of the fanciful drawings made in the Dark Ages, with Jerusalem at the earth's centre and the Garden of Eden on its edge, excellent charts, called 'Portulani', had been produced, very accurate for the Mediterranean and its neighbourhood but in-increasingly vague and speculative for regions further away. Moreover, the slow wobbling of the earth's axis had brought the north pole of the sky, the point round which the whole sky seems to revolve, nearer and nearer to one brightish star, Polaris at the tail-end of the Little Bear.

Henry consulted shipbuilders and cartographers, makers of mathematical instruments, and far-travelled seamen. He also consulted astronomers, mathematicians and other scientists, for he knew the help which the men of theory can give to the practical men. His court became a school of navigation, where the seafarers and the scientists could learn from one another.

It was in his shipyards that a new type of vessel was designed, the caravel, suited either for coasting or for putting out into the deep. Based on the type of fishing-vessel or trader used on the Portuguese coast, she was light, not more than two hundred tons, with her bows streamlined to cleave the water. She had two or more masts, and was rigged partly with square sails and partly with lateen sails (resembling those used on Arab dhows), so that she could sail close to the wind.

So Henry had his ships, his navigational instruments, and his charts—very reliable so far as the knowledge of the time went—as well as his experts. What he now needed was seamen skilful and brave enough to sail, so to speak, off the edge of the map.

Here he found unexpected difficulties, for the most horrific stories had spread about the mysterious regions south of the known world. The limit of this was Cape Bojador, on the north-west coast of Africa; it was supposed to be so swept by dangerous currents and trade-winds that nobody foolhardy enough to pass it could ever get back. And beyond the Cape, so the rumour ran, the heat became so great that the land would be parched and uninhabitable, and the very sea would boil; indeed to push on further would be to risk having one's skin burned completely—and permanently—black.

Even the ancient writings then so much valued were conflicting. Ptolemy's map showed South Africa as trending eastwards and uniting with China, while on the other hand Herodotus spoke of seamen who had actually sailed round Africa. Plainly the only way of discovering the truth was to go and see.

Henry's duties prevented him from going; his work was not to explore, but to organize exploration. He encouraged seamen to cruise as far as they could down the African coast, and to bring back not only careful records of their travels but also specimens from whatever strange lands they reached—soil and rocks, plants and animals—and any human inhabitants who could be induced or made to come.

Some of his sea-captains sailed a little way down the coast to please him until their faith or their nerve failed and they turned back. Instead of coasting Africa they entered the Mediterranean for the more exciting and profitable task of raiding the Moors. But others had stouter hearts, and were ready to venture into the unknown; the reports and observations which they brought back were carefully recorded on the maps.

Their courage was well rewarded. In 1418 two adventurers, Zarco and Vaz, were driven by a storm on to an unknown island, which they called Porto Santo. So pleasant was it that they gladly returned to colonize it; but unfortunately they took with them a few rabbits, which soon multiplied to such an extent that they devastated the island's vegetation.

Undiscouraged, the explorers set out to investigate a dark spot visible on the horizon from Porto Santo. To their delight it was a much larger island, fertile, well wooded, well watered, and attractive in every way. But they found they were not the first to reach it, for near the ruins of a shanty was a cross with an inscription saying that 'here came Machin, an Englishman, driven by the tempest, and here lies buried Anna d'Arfet'.

The two explorers called this island Madeira, the 'Island of Woods', and when Henry rewarded them by dividing it between them they called half of it Machico, after the unknown Englishman who had forestalled them. Though devastated by a forest fire, Madeira soon recovered, and became a flourishing colony, exporting many articles, including a famous wine and possibly the timber from which the first caravels were built.

The stores about the intense heat beyond Cape Bojador might have been absurd, but the difficulties about returning round in the face of adverse currents and winds were very real. However, it might be possible to circumvent them by sailing well out to sea, beyond the Canaries. Here the explorers could not get their bearings from the land; they would have to get them from the sun or the stars, and the experts at Henry's court showed them how this could be done.

Armed with this knowledge, an experienced sea-man, Concalho Velho, set out to seek for the 'Lost Islands' rumoured to exist out in the Atlantic. Possibly about 1429 he found them, and they too were as fertile and as easily colonized as Madeira itself. They are the Azores, named after the falcons said to be living on them when they were found.

It took twelve years before Cape Bojador was rounded, in 1434, by Gil Eannes. True, the coast beyond was not very attractive, being mostly desert with only a few stunted shrubs. Yet Henry welcomed specimens of these when Eannes brought them back in triumph. It showed that the Cape, so long supposed to be the limit of possible travel, could be passed without overmuch danger, and that the horror stories were untrue.

Now expedition after expedition went further and further down the African coast. When in 1441 Gonsalves and Tristram reached Cape Blanco and returned with some gold-dust and some negro prisoners, exploration grew popular, for slaves were almost as valuable as gold.

Beyond Cape Blanco the desert conditions passed into country so fertile that the next of the African headlands, reached in 1446, was called Cape Verde (green). Between the two capes was the mouth of a river, so large and with its shores so thickly wooded that the explorers decided it must be the western mouth of the Nile, though the natives called it Senegal.

Among the seamen who came from far and wide to offer their services to Henry was a young Venetian, Cadamosto, who had a passionate desire to explore the unknown. In 1455 he went up the Senegal for about two hundred and fifty miles. When he set up a market to barter cloth for gold, the natives clamoured round him, marvelling at his clothing and especially at his white colour, which they vainly tried to wash off.

Returning to the coast, he cruised on beyond Cape Verde, to a point so far south that the North Star was so low in the sky that it almost touched the sea. Finding that on those shores the natives were fierce, and that there was little gold, he turned homewards, and during his voyage he discovered the Cape Verde Islands.

Three years later Diego Gomez went even further, to the mouth of the Gambia. Here, he learned, there was gold in plenty, and here too there was trade with the Mohammedans of Northern Africa. He was able to get on friendly terms with the natives, and even to convert one of their kings.

Henry was naturally overjoyed to hear this, and followed up this missionary work by sending a priest out to the newly-converted king. This was the last expedition which he organized, for two years later, in 1460, he died.

Prince Henry was dead, but his work lived on. Thanks to the advances in navigation which he had made possible, other explorers were able to push on further down the African coast into the unknown. In 1461 they reached Sierra Leone, the furthest point attained centuries before by Hanno of Carthage. When in 1471 they crossed the Equator, they were astonished to find that the Pole Star had sunk below the horizon and that new star-patterns had come into sight.

Now, however, they met with disappointment. Beyond Sierra Leone the land trended eastward so far that they must have thought they had reached the southernmost part of Africa. At the Bight of Benin, however, it trended south again, and it seemed to stretch endlessly on.

Unperturbed, the explorers pushed on southwards; thanks to Prince Henry they had lost their fear of the unknown. In 1482 Diego Cam embarked on a voyage in which he discovered the mouth of the Congo; sailing upstream, he made friends with the natives and persuaded some of them to accompany him to Portugal. They were so kindly treated that when he took them back in 1485 their king and queen and many of their people were converted. On his second voyage he reached Cape Cross, about 20° south of the Equator, having discovered 1450 miles of a difficult and dangerous coast.

Enquiries made in India having suggested that it was possible to sail there round Africa, in 1487

Bartholomew Diaz attempted to reach it. Passing the Congo, he surveyed the coast as far as Walfisch Bay, but so difficult were the off-shore currents that he had then to sail southwards out of sight of land. After a time the winds drove him first eastwards, then northwards, taking him to a strange coast, Mossel Bay, which he recognized as an unknown part of Africa.

With some difficulty, due both to the heavy seas and to the hostile natives, he sailed along the coast, until its continual north-easterly trend convinced him that he was actually beyond the southernmost point of Africa. At the Great Fish River his crew refused to sail further; so, with bitter regret, Diaz bade farewell to the cross he had erected on Santa Cruz Island and turned homewards. During the journey he discovered and rounded the Cape of Good Hope.

A good hope it was, indeed, for those whose aim was to reach India. The attempt was made in 1497 by Vasco da Gama, with four ships and 118 men, and with the finest maps and books and scientific instruments which could be obtained.

From the Cape Verde Islands he sailed southwards, on a route which may have taken him nearer to South America than to Africa, and then eastward. After spending over ninety days out of sight of land, he reached the African coast at what he called St. Helena Bay. Having rounded the Cape, in weather so stormy that the crew and even the pilot clamoured to go back, he sailed to Mossel Bay, where he was able to get supplies of fresh meat, and to the Great Fish River.

Beyond this all was unexplored. Favoured by the wind and current, da Gama cruised along the African coast, calling part of it Natal because he reached it on Christmas Day. Then he stood some distance out to sea, until shortage of food and water drove him to seek land once more. He and his men were much cheered by reaching the broad Quilimane River, which they called the 'River of Good Tokens', for here the natives were not only friendly but said that they had seen large ships similar to his. As these must have come from the opposite direction, he was obviously within reach of civilization.

Here da Gama had to wait for a month taking in water and careening and repairing his ships. But now came a disaster worse even than the hardships and perils he and his men had already endured: they were afflicted by scurvy, a dreadful disease now known to be due to vitamin-lack. Their hands and feet became swollen, their teeth fell out, and their gums grew so far over their teeth that they could hardly eat.

Yet even this did not deter da Gama, who insisted on travelling on up the coast. Off Mozambique he encountered some Arab dhows, trading in spices and precious stones with the natives. The Arabs, to put it mildly, did not welcome him, and it was only with difficulty and in the face of great danger that he reached Melindi, where a friendly king supplied him with food

D

and whence a pilot took his ships across the Indian Ocean to Calcutta.

Here again he was unwelcome, for the Moslems wanted to keep the valuable spice trade to themselves. Nonetheless, da Gama found that the prospects for trade were excellent, and he collected much useful information about their regions further east. Greatly rejoicing, he decided to return to Portugal. After severe losses from another attack of scurvy, and after having to abandon one of his ships, he arrived safely at Lisbon, where he received a tumultuous welcome. He had travelled about twenty-four thousand miles, and had been away over six hundred days, half of them right out at sea.

Da Gama made two more journeys to South India and soon a number of other Portuguese seafarers were following him. These journeys led to the discovery and exploration not only of other regions in the Far East, but also of two islands, hitherto unknown, in the Atlantic: Ascension and St. Helena.

It was the work of Prince Henry of Portugal which had made these achievements possible. Though he himself travelled little, he did so much to encourage and develop seafaring that he has always been known as Henry the Navigator. Similarly, though he personally made no discoveries, he did so much to encourage and foster the investigation of foreign lands that he might just as well be called Henry the Explorer.

Compared with the exploits of Hanno, Pharaoh

Necho's Carthaginians, and the Vikings, the slow advance of Henry's sea-captains down the African coast might seem over-cautious and unenterprising. Yet its results were far more important, preparing the way for Diaz and da Gama. The coastal voyages of Hanno and Necho's Phoenicians, and the Vikings' light-hearted dash across the Atlantic, achieved little; but Henry the Navigator and his seamen changed the whole course of history.

11 New World in the West

WHILE some of the explorers were making their way down the African coast, others were cruising westward. Some returned declaring that they had sighted unknown islands; others brought back pieces of wood found floating in the sea, coming from unfamiliar trees and artificially cut. Rumours of land beyond the Atlantic began to spread.

Among those who took the rumours seriously was the Nuremberg geographer, Martin Behaim. His own experience with a Portuguese expedition down the African coast had made him realize the need for accurate charts, and he became noted for his new methods of finding latitude at sea, for his maps, and especially for his great globe of the earth. On this he showed several imaginary islands, Brandan, Antilla, and Brazil, and east of the Chinese coast he showed a whole archipelago.

The rumours were taken even more seriously by a seaman named Christopher Columbus. The extent of his early travels is uncertain: they ranged from the East to Britain and possibly to Iceland. After much thought, he made up his mind to undertake a mighty project.

Like all knowledgeable people of his time, he knew that the earth is a sphere, and he realized more clearly than others that because of this lands east of Europe are also west of Europe—the other way round. Like Ptolemy, he under-estimated the size of the earth and over-estimated that of Asia, so he thought that the rich lands described by Marco Polo in the Far East could not be so very far in the West. The Italian astronomer whom he consulted, Paolo Toscanelli, agreed that he was right.

Only a monarch could send an expedition to find them, and the one most likely to do so was the King of Portugal, so it was from him that Columbus first sought aid. Henry the Navigator might have been enthusiastic for such a project; but he was dead, and the experts who advised John II of Portugal were too intent on their own plan for reaching India round Africa to welcome a rival scheme for seeking it across the Atlantic. King John did, however, make a half-hearted effort to carry out Columbus' plan without Columbus' help, but this scheme met with the failure it deserved: the crews mutinied, the captain lost heart, and the expedition returned shamefacedly.

Columbus next applied to the rulers of Spain; but they were too busy driving the Moors out of their country to undertake adventures overseas. He then sent his brother Bartholomew to appeal to Henry VII of England; but England was not yet a maritime country, and he got no support here.

Year upon year of fruitless effort and disappointment did not discourage Columbus. It was not only a matter of getting the rich Eastern trade, he explained eagerly. It meant that the peoples of distant lands could be converted to the Christian faith; it meant an alliance with Prester John to drive the heathen from the Holy Land and regain Jerusalem. His earnestness impressed influential people, wealthy tradesmen and nobles, and Church leaders.

Supported by them, he went back to the Spanish Court; and now, the Moors having been defeated, he was heard more favourably. Queen Isabella, a deeply-religious woman, was stirred by the enthusiasm with which he explained his hopes of converting the heathen. Unreasonable though they sounded, his demands were impressive: he must be admiral in command of the expedition and Viceroy of the lands it discovered, and receive a tenth of any gold or silver it found.

So at last, on 3rd August 1492, Columbus set sail. His three ships, the 100-ton *Santa Maria* and two smaller caravels, the *Pinta* and *Nina*, were manned by a mixed crew, less than ninety in all, of seamen, adventurers, and jail-birds released specially to accompany him. They sailed first to the Canaries and then westwards into the unknown.

Day after day, week after week, they cruised onward, and still there were no signs of land. Food and water showed signs of running short. The compass began to act so erratically that even the seamen were scared, and Columbus himself got nervous; the landlubbers were thoroughly panic-stricken, fearing they might sail on for ever, or plunge right off the edge of the world. They threatened mutiny and pleaded to be taken back before it was too late. Columbus refused; he was unmoved by their pleas and undaunted by their threats.

At last came signs that reassured even the fainthearted: some birds, a piece of wood showing tool markings, a branch bearing unfamiliar berries. In the darkness a light gleamed ahead, and next day, the 12th October, Columbus landed on an unknown shore and took possession of it in the name of King Ferdinand and Queen Isabella of Spain.

Where he actually made his landfall is uncertain—probably on Watling Island, in the Bahamas. Other islands lay nearby, and beyond them he reached a larger island (Cuba); this, he decided, must be Cipangu (Japan). While exploring it and collecting its rarities and making friends with its people he discovered something new to Europe—the tobacco plant.

Soon he realized his mistake: the island he had

reached was not Cipangu, but he thought another (Haiti) must be; he called it Espanola in honour of the Spanish monarchs. Leaving a small colony there, he returned, by way of the Azores, to Spain.

He was received with high honour. He had shown that the Atlantic could be crossed, that beyond it were strange lands to explore, strange beasts and birds, and, most surprising of all, strange races of men. News of his achievement spread over Europe, and in many countries adventurers set out to seek their fortunes across the sea.

One of these was Columbus himself. On 25th September 1493 he sailed with a much larger expedition, intending to reinforce his colony and to explore further. Having discovered several other islands, including the Leeward Group, he at last reached Haiti.

Here, however, disappointment awaited him, for his colony had been wiped out by the natives. This, too, was only the beginning of strife between them and the Europeans, for this attitude towards these 'heathen' was hardening and he thought that they would make good slaves. Having founded another colony, Isabella, and sent prospectors to look for gold in the mountains, he went on to Cuba; this, he now decided, was not an island, but part of the Asiatic mainland. Fearing that the colonists on Isabella would make trouble for him at court, in 1495 he returned to Spain.

Again he was received with honour, and in 1498 he made another expedition. On this he discovered not only another island, Trinidad, but—though he did not realize this—the South American mainland. But the colonists on Haiti accused him of misgovernment, arrested him and sent him home in chains.

Released and restored to royal favour, in 1503 Columbus made a fourth voyage. He now regarded the islands he had found as barring the route to Asia, and he was anxious to find some passage between them. Having explored the Gulf of Mexico and reached the coast of Honduras, he returned to Spain neither honoured nor disgraced, but simply disregarded; there he died, unhappy and neglected, in 1506.

The Portuguese now understood how unwise they had been in not supporting Columbus, and in letting Spain get the first foothold on the transatlantic shore. They resolved to make up for the lost opportunity, and it may have been this resolve which spurred on da Gama to reach India by way of the Cape.

Columbus was convinced that he had reached Asia. Because of this misunderstanding, the islands he had reached were—and still are—called the Indies, the term West Indies being used to distinguish them from the East Indies of Asia. The geographers, however, first suspected and then realized that what he had actually discovered was not part of Asia but some new continent, hitherto unknown and undreamed of.

In 1501 the Portuguese king employed an Italian seaman, Amerigo Vespucci, to explore the lands beyond the Atlantic. He had already crossed it twice: on his first voyage he had reached the coast of Mexico, and on the second that of South America.

Now, on his third and greatest voyage, he explored the South American coast from a little below the Equator right down to Patagonia, a distance of nearly four thousand miles. So amazing was this achievement, and so clearly did it prove that what lay across the Atlantic was a continent so large it might be called a New World, that it gained him an honour which might well have gone to the earlier explorer. It is not from Columbus but from Amerigo that America gets its name.

Now that Spain and Portugal both had a foothold in the New World, the risks of a clash between them were obvious. Pope Alexander VI had already foreseen this, and in 1494 he had decreed that there should be a frontier along the meridian 370 leagues west of the Cape Verde Islands. East of this, all newly-discovered lands were to belong to Portugal; west of it, to Spain.

While letting Portugal have a free hand in Africa and Asia, this seemed to give Spain the whole of the New World. Then it was found that part of South America was actually east of this line, and so belonged to Portugal. So a great region called Brazil, after one of Behaim's imaginary islands, became Portuguese, while the rest of South America, as well as Mexico and Central America, formed part of the Spanish Empire. This accounts for the languages still spoken in these lands.

It was one thing for the Pope to divide much of the

world between Spain and Portugal, but quite another to get the other nations to agree. Like the Portuguese, the English realized their mistake in not supporting Columbus, and, Roman Catholics though they were, they too decided to make up for lost time.

For some time the Bristol merchants, whose Icelandic trade in salt and fish was falling off, had been sending expeditions to find the island of Brazil. So they were ready to listen to an Italian seaman, John Cabot, when he approached them with a scheme for sailing westwards to Asia. He explained that at Mecca there was a great trade in spices, which were said to have been brought by a series of long journeys from far in the East. As the earth was round, the regions from which the spices came could not be so very far in the West.

In 1496 Henry VII authorized Cabot and his sons to explore and take possession of any unknown regions bordering 'the Eastern, Western and Northern sea'. This avoided a clash with the Spanish, but it meant that the Cabots had to traverse the stormy North Atlantic, a more difficult and dangerous voyage than that of Columbus.

During his first voyage, made in 1497, Cabot reached either Nova Scotia or Newfoundland, where he explored the coasts. Like Columbus, he too mistook them for part of Asia: he thought they were north of China. This discovery, that land could be reached across the North Atlantic, was important enough to justify his second voyage, in 1498, when he may have prospected the

American coast as far south as Delaware. Though Cabot, like Columbus, failed to reach Asia, and though he did not plant any colonies in the 'New Found Land' he had discovered, he disclosed to the seamen of Europe the rich fishing-grounds off its coast.

12 Conquering the New World

THE Spaniards soon realized that they need not regret having failed to find a new route to wealthy Asia; the New World they had discovered was wealthier still. It offered them lands to colonize, populations to enslave, civilizations to conquer, as well as glory and power, and plenty of loot. Though they might find but little gold, they kept hearing rumours of regions where it abounded. Old half-forgotten legends were revived: stories about El Dorado, 'The Land of Gold', and of the Fountain of Youth, a spring whose waters kept anyone who drank them from ever getting old.

Only a few romantic adventurers took this Fountain very seriously. Juan Ponce de Leon, who had accompanied Columbus on his second voyage, set out to find it. Needless to say, he failed; but the quest led him, in 1513, to discover what he thought was an island, which he called Florida ('Flower Land'). Without realizing it, he had reached the North American mainland.

The quest for El Dorado led the Conquistadors (conquerors), as they called themselves, ever further inland from their coastal settlements. Nothing daunted them: trackless forests and swamps, great rivers, steep mountain-slopes covered with a chaos of rocks, snakes large enough to swallow a man whole, tiny fish who could devour him piecemeal, fierce animals, and even fiercer savages, as vindictive as they were treacherous.

Some of the rumours led them nowhere, for the natives found it was no use telling a Conquistador athirst for gold that they had none: the thing to do was to tell him that of course there was gold, plenty of gold, some distance further on—and hope that when he went to find it he would never come back.

This quest, however, led Vasco Nuñez de Balboa to make a discovery as important as that of America. In Darien (Eastern Panama) a friendly chief, amazed at the value the Spaniards set on gold, told him that beside the mighty sea beyond the mountains it was as common as iron.

Balboa set off to cross those mountains. When, in 1513, after great hardship and peril, he reached their summit he saw in the distance an unknown sea: he was the first European to sight the Pacific.

Descending to the shore, he waded out in full armour to claim what he called the South Sea and its shores for Spain, and to embark on its waters. With incredible labour he had two ships dragged across the Isthmus of Panama, and with them he explored the coast, discovered the Pearl Islands in the Gulf of Panama, and almost reached the coast of Peru.

When, in 1517, explorers from Cuba landed on Yucatán they heard of a great civilization, whose capital, a city in a lake miles to the west, abounded in treasure. Two years later an expedition set out to reach and conquer this city; its leader, Hernando Cortéz, founded a seaport, Vera Cruz, to serve as his base while he advanced inland. His ambition was to be a modern Alexander the Great.

The civilization he sought was that of the Aztecs of Mexico. Though advanced and cultured in many ways, with a marvellous system of picture-writing, the Aztecs were warlike and cruel, dominating large populations and making human sacrifices to their bloodthirsty gods. They had a prophecy that a god would come to them from over the sea, and at first they fancied that Cortéz might be that god.

Because of that prophecy, which made their resistance half-hearted; of their reluctance to kill their enemies, for they wanted prisoners to sacrifice; of their fear of horsemen, which they took to be centaur-like monsters; and of the hate which their subject peoples had for them, the Aztecs were overcome by Cortéz and his army of a few hundred men. By a combination of daring and treachery he captured the Aztec king Montezuma, and conquered and plundered Mexico City.

He then sent his followers to explore the land he had won and to found new cities. Westwards, they reached the coast and founded seaports on the Pacific; northwards, they reached California and Texas; southwards, they reached Guatemala and Honduras. Thus within a few years the Spaniards had conquered all Central

America, and secured a foothold in the great regions
to its north and south.

Soon the Conquistadors heard of another wealthy
civilization further south. Its existence was verified by
Fernando Pizarro, who in 1524 began a three-year
exploration of South America; having forced his way
through swamps and flooded waste-lands where most
of his men perished, he found beyond the Equator a
civilized people, some of whom wore gold ornaments.

Authorized by his government to conquer and rule
any lands he might reach, Pizarro landed, in 1532, at
Tumbez in the north of Peru. Like Cortéz, whose
methods he was adopting, he founded a city—San
Miguel—to serve as his base while he advanced into the
unknown.

The Incas who ruled Peru had a civilization as strange
as that of the Aztecs. Without machines, and even without mortar, they had erected great buildings; without
iron, they were skilled in using tools of bronze and
copper; without any form of writing—they kept their
accounts by means of knotted cords—they were advanced in astronomy.

As in Mexico, some of their subject peoples resented
their rule and were ready to welcome the Spanish
invaders. When these arrived, in 1532, the Incas themselves were divided by a civil war. Taking advantage
of this, Pizarro, with a force of less than two hundred
men, crossed the Andes in spite of the intense cold.
Combining daring with treachery, like Cortéz, he

conquered the Inca capital, Cuzco, and made himself master of all Peru.

Again like Mexico, this new Spanish colony became a centre from which explorers could set out. Some went northwards into and beyond Equador, where they met other Spanish expeditions coming from the coast up the Magdalena River in search of El Dorado. Some went southwards into Chile as far as the Chiloé archipelago; but here instead of a wealthy civilization they found only fierce Indian tribes.

Some were better rewarded, for when they crossed the Andes into Bolivia, in 1545, they discovered the rich silver-mines of Potosi. Some went right down a mighty river to the sea; encountering some warlike Indian women along its banks, their leader, Francisco de Orellana, remembered a race of women-warriors described by the Ancient Greeks, and called the river the Amazon.

North America was also explored. In 1528 Panfilo de Narvaez landed in Florida, with authority to conquer and rule all the country as far as Mexico. Marching somewhat inland, he lost touch with his fleet; and though he constructed boats, his expedition met with disaster. One of its few survivors who reached the mainland, Cabeza de Vaca, lived for five years among the natives. After travelling northwards to the Colorado River he turned southwards to Mexico, the first European to cross North America from sea to sea.

Returning to Spain, he described the American

plants and animals, including the bison, and praised
the keen senses and the hardihood of the Red Indians.
His narrative helped another Conquistador, Hernando
de Soto, to make a large-scale exploration, from
Georgia to the Appalachian Mountains and the
Alabama River. Having discovered the Mississippi and
vainly tried to find a route seawards to its west, he
turned south, but in the great riverside swamps he died
of fever. Though threatened with starvation, his successor, Luis de Moscoso, succeeded in bringing the
remnants of the expedition safely down the Mississippi
by boat.

De Vaca and an imaginative friar, Marcos de Niza,
extolled the wealth of North America. Niza, who had
travelled in Arizona and New Mexico, mentioned what
he called 'the Seven Cities of Cibola' as being especially
rich, but when an expedition led by Francisco Vasquez
de Coronado reached them they were found to be little
more than one overcrowded village. This fiasco seems
to have been blamed on Coronado; but though he had
failed to find any gold, his expedition had accomplished
much.

It revealed to the Spaniards the vast unknown region
north of Mexico, the great plains, the bison which
teemed on the plains and the Indian tribes which lived
by hunting the bison. But what most impressed the
explorers was the Grand Canyon of Colorado, which
seemed nearly ten miles from cliff-top to cliff-top, and
was so deep that the river below, though half a league
wide, looked as if it were only six feet across.

Thus all Central America, most of South America, and the southern part of North America now belonged to the Spanish Empire, while the Portuese had gained Brazil as well as their settlements in Asia. Unfortunately these conquests involved much suffering and cruelty. The Conquistadors plundered the rich civilizations of the New World and ill-treated and sometimes enslaved its people, while the Portuguese were brutal and treacherous in the Far East. Their leaders quarrelled bitterly and attacked one another with false accusations. Columbus, sent home in chains, was only one of the sufferers; Cortéz, whom the Spanish king did not wish to reward but who was too popular for him to punish, was humiliated by neglect and scorn; Balboa, condemned on a trumped-up charge, was executed.

Presently Spanish and Portuguese alike had new enemies to contend with, the buccaneers from England, France, and then Holland. Though later they won small colonies in Guiana, there was little that these newcomers could do on land; for his failure to reach El Dorado, Sir Walter Raleigh was beheaded. But there was much they could do at sea, intercepting and plundering the treasure-ships which brought the wealth of America to Spain or raiding the ports from which it was sent.

In the long run this wealth did little good to the Spanish. Some was squandered by those who gained it. Some went to the rulers of Spain and brought that poverty-struck land a temporary prosperity; but it too was squandered in the fruitless attempt of Philip II to keep the Netherlands, then part of the Spanish Empire, from gaining their independence, and to conquer England with the Spanish Armada.

Fortunately, the Conquistadors were not the only Spaniards to reach America. They were soon followed by such missionaries as Las Casas, who instead of enslaving and oppressing the South Americans sought to protect and benefit them. Thanks to the monks, and also to far-sighted and conscientious rulers, the position of the natives was greatly improved. The Aztec and Inca civilizations had been destroyed, but in their place rose a new civilization which, though not perfect, was at any rate free from such horrors as human sacrifice. Its people were mostly of South American descent, but its rulers, and its outlook and culture, were Spanish or Portuguese, while its religion was Roman Catholic.

The missionaries continued the work of exploration, and at last the Americas, at first rather vaguely and inaccurately, found their place upon the world map.

13 Voyage around the World

THOUGH it was a new world to colonize, America was also a barrier between Europe and the Far East; so, much as Columbus had sought for a passage between the West Indies, the Spanish seamen sought for a gap in this immense continent. Rumours were spreading that there was such a gap far down to its south, and Charles V of Spain was prepared to listen to an experienced seaman who sought to find it.

Portuguese by birth, Ferdinand Magellan had lost favour with his own king, and had no qualms about offering his services to another monarch. In spite of protests from Portugal, Charles authorized him to discover any unexplored regions in the Spanish half of the world, west of the line fixed by the Pope, but enjoined him strictly not to trespass upon the Portuguese half east of that line. (The two would, of course, meet somewhere in the East Indies, and it was not certain in which half the Spice Islands lay.)

Sailing in September 1519 with a flotilla of five rather second-rate ships, Magellan was delayed by bad weather in the Atlantic, and the onset of the Southern winter forced him to shelter in Port St. Julian, which Vespucci had discovered. The hardships of wintering on reduced rations led his captains to plot his assassination, but by a combination of firmness and mercy he was able to quell the attempted mutiny.

A ship he had sent to explore the coast southwards was wrecked in a storm, and the crew had to return overland. Then the members of the expedition were surprised to see, on a coast which they had thought uninhabited, a 'giant' who to their startled eyes looked twice as tall as a man. He was clad only in skins, and his fur boots were so badly made that his people have ever since been called the Patagonians ('large clumsy feet').

When warm weather returned, the explorers spent two months replenishing their supplies of dried fish and firewood. Soon, on 21st October 1520, they found, as though by miracle, the gap they were looking for, a narrow strait a little beyond the furthest point reached by Vespucci.

The gap led westwards, and a scouting party brought the good tidings that on its far side it opened into the sea. Though these Straits of Magellan are only a few hundred miles long, it took their discoverer over a month to traverse them (and one of his ships, sent to explore a side-channel, simply waited till the others had passed and then deserted and made for home).

The open sea beyond the Straits was so calm that Magellan called it the Pacific ('peaceful') Ocean. Calm though it was, however, it seemed endless, and for ninety-eight days the three ships sailed on, so short of supplies that the crews had to drink putrid water and to eat biscuits crumbling to dust and full of weevils, ox-hide from the masts needing several days' soaking in sea-water before it could be toasted and eaten, sawdust, and rats; they suffered, and many of them died, not only from hunger and thirst, but also from scurvy and other diseases.

Not until January 1521 did they reach land, Puka Puka in the Paumoto Archipelago. Later they found another island group; and this, because the natives stole his skiff, Magellan called the Ladrones ('thieves')—now better known as the Marianas.

In April the expedition reached yet another group, the Philippines; but here, unfortunately, Magellan got involved in a native quarrel, and he and a number of his men were slain.

Though forced to abandon another of their ships, and bereft of their skilful and courageous leader, the Spaniards carried on his work. Reaching Borneo, where they found a city, Brunei, built on piles above the water, they were welcomed by the Sultan; but they were suspicious of treachery and sailed on to the Moluccas. Here they took on board a cargo of the spices they had come half-way round the world to find.

One of their ships, the *Trinity*, was too badly in need of repair to continue the long journey, and it too had to be abandoned. Only one vessel, the *Victoria*, was left to sail for home, and she ran short of food, for her captain, Sebastian del Cano, had to keep clear of land for fear of conflict with the Portuguese. At the Cape Verde Islands, indeed, the men he sent ashore were arrested; and only eighteen completed the voyage by returning to Spain. For the first time the world had been circumnavigated; the voyage had taken a little under three years.

Even the *Trinity*, the vessel left behind in the Moluccas, gained information useful to seamen. Though her attempt to return to America failed, the course she followed, well to the north of Magellan's route, showed how very large the Pacific is.

Other discoveries soon followed. The Spaniards may have reached the Sandwich Islands in 1527, and in 1565 they began to colonize the Philippines. In that year, too, Andres de Urdaneta, by cruising well to the north of the westerly trade-winds, succeeded in crossing the Pacific from west to east.

The route Andres de Urdaneta followed, since called 'Urdaneta's passage', enabled the Spaniards to keep their American colonies in touch with their islands in the Pacific. Later they discovered some other islands, but for some time they and the Portuguese were too busy tracing and developing their colonies to attempt further exploration.

The reason the Portuguese wanted to intercept the remnants of Magellan's expedition was that they were anxious to keep the Eastern trade to themselves; and the aim of that expedition was to give the Spanish a share in that valuable trade.

Plainly the risks of a clash between the two nations

were greater in the Far East even than they had been in the West. To prevent this, the frontier fixed by the Pope was extended through the Poles and right across the Pacific.

As before, the other nations of Europe cared little for this decision, especially when the Reformation made the English and the Dutch throw off any allegiance to the Pope. Soon they too were seeking a share in the Eastern trade.

England was not only Protestant, but moreover on bad terms with Spain, when, in November 1577, Francis Drake sailed from Plymouth. After capturing some Spanish and Portuguese vessels off the West African coast, Drake headed for Brazil. Like Magellan, he had a flotilla of five ships; like Magellan, he wintered in Port St. Julian; and here, again like Magellan, he was able to quell a threatened mutiny.

When, in the following September, he traversed the Straits of Magellan, he encountered bad weather in the Pacific. This drove him to what he called 'the southern-most knowne land in the world', the storm-swept Cape Horn. Though deserted by his other ships, he continued the voyage in his own vessel, the *Golden Hind*, following the western coast of South America and noticing that it had been very inaccurately mapped. At Valparaiso he captured a Spanish ship, and having thus replenished his stores he sailed on to North America. Here he found a 'faire and good' harbour, San Francisco Bay; as the Spanish did not seem to have come so far north, he called this country New Albion, and claimed it for his queen.

Having crossed the Pacific by a route more northerly than Magellan's, Drake reached the Moluccas, where he made a favourable treaty with the natives. Later his ship ran upon a rock and was grounded for eight hours until a change in the wind refloated her.

At Java Drake took on board a valuable cargo of spices, and he returned round the Cape of Good Hope to England. Here he was knighted by Elizabeth I, not only for being the first of her subjects to circumnavigate the earth but also because he had gained for her country a share in the Eastern trade.

In 1588 another Englishman, Thomas Cavendish, had circumnavigated the world; otherwise he accomplished little except to raid the Spanish. What the latter found more alarming was the arrival in the Pacific of the Dutch, who were not only seeking trade but were still embittered by the attempts of Philip II to subdue them.

The first Dutch expedition to the Pacific, in 1598, was commanded by James Mahu, but before he could traverse the Straits of Magellan his ships were scattered by a storm. One reached the Falkland Islands and another island group much further south, probably the South Shetlands.

Another ship, the *Charity*, passed through the Straits and crossed the Pacific to Japan; her pilot, William Adams, was the first Englishman the Japanese had seen, and they found his knowledge of shipbuilding and seamanship so useful that they refused to allow him to leave. Having married a Japanese girl, Adams seems to have made the best of things, and to have settled down fairly happily.

14 Quest for a Northern Passage

WHEN John Cabot crossed the North Atlantic, he hoped to find what was called the North-West Passage, around the north coast of the newly-discovered continent, to Asia. In 1509 his son Sebastian Cabot continued the search; he found a hopeful-looking strait which opened into a large sea, but ice and discontent among his crew prevented him from exploring it—he had probably traversed Hudson Strait into Hudson Bay. Later, as Henry VIII refused him further help, he entered the Spanish service.

Other attempts were made to discover the North-West Passage, but they were unsuccessful. Meantime the waters off Newfoundland were getting better known, for they were attracting many fishermen, including a number from Brittany.

In 1534 the Breton seaman Jacques Cartier visited those waters, not to fish but to seek the North-West Passage. Though hindered by ice, he succeeded in entering Belle Isle Strait, between Newfoundland and Labrador, whose coast was so barren that he thought it might be 'the land God gave to Cain': though it possessed good harbours it consisted not of earth but of 'stones and horrible rugged rocks'. Turning south-wards, he found several small islands and a larger one, Prince Edward Island; unlike Labrador, this had every-thing except good harbours.

Continuing his investigation, he found what looked like a bay but was really Northumberland Strait, and then what looked like a strait but was really Chaleur Bay; next, an opening which he mistook for another large bay, north of Anticosti Island. Cartier tried to enter this to see whether it were a bay or a strait, but the current was so strong he could make no headway. So, urged by his officers and crew, he returned to France.

Next year he made a second voyage to complete his exploration. Again he traversed Belle Isle Strait. Now, after consulting some friendly Indians, who explained that what he had mistaken for a bay was really a great river-mouth, he sailed up the St. Lawrence.

Still welcomed by the Indians, he cruised far up-stream, to their capital Hochelaga, the site of the modern Montreal. Here there was a lofty hill, Mount

Royal, after which that city is named, and from its summit he got a splendid view of 'the finest land it is possible to see', stretching endlessly into the distance. When the violent Lachine Rapids prevented his going further, he gained information from his friends the Indians about the country beyond.

The expedition wintered at the St. Charles River, near Quebec, and here it was ravaged by scurvy. The Indians told him of a remedy made from the leaves of a tree, probably the hemlock-spruce; his men were at first unwilling to use it, but when they found how good it was they fought to get it.

On his homeward journey Cartier found a much broader opening than the narrow Belle Isle Strait: Cabot Strait to the South of Newfoundland. Though he had failed to find the North-West Passage, his work later enabled the French to colonize the great land to which he had given the Indian name for village: Canada.

When Sebastian Cabot returned to England in 1548 he was regarded as an authority on navigation in the northern seas. By his advice the Muscovy Company was formed. Its aim was not only to trade with Russia, but to discover any unknown regions, and if possible to send vessels to China not by the North-West Passage, but by a North-East Passage round the Russian coast.

In May 1553 Sir Hugh Willoughby and Richard Chancelor headed an expedition up the Norwegian coast. They were separated by a storm, and though

Willoughby and his men managed to reach Lapland, they had suffered so badly that they died.

Chancelor continued his voyage, the midnight sun enabling him to enter the White Sea. Thence he travelled overland to Moscow, where he made a favourable trade agreement and gained much useful information about Russia and its people.

The Dutch were deeply interested in these ventures, for they were anxious to share in the profitable trade with Russia. They sent out several expeditions, the most successful being made by William Barentz. On his first two voyages he too sought for the North-East Passage along the Russian coast.

On his third voyage, in 1596, he followed a more westerly course, sailing almost due north towards the Pole. This course led him to Bear Island, where a landing party almost came to grief on the slippery ice.

Further north he sighted a much larger island, which he thought was part of Greenland, though it was really Spitzbergen. He was astonished at its fertility, for although lands further south had been almost barren, it was covered with grass and trees and it harboured deer.

Barentz did not land on Spitzbergen, but turned eastwards to Novaya Zemlya, where his ship was frozen in. This was the first time any expedition had wintered in the Arctic, so he and his men had no records of earlier explorers to guide them; they had to learn from bitter experience.

Their ship was partly crushed by the ice, but what

they regarded as a providential find of driftwood enabled them to build a hut and to lay in a store of fuel.
They needed this, too, for their hut was almost buried
by the snow. Though within it they were almost suffo-
cated by the smoke and fumes, when they ventured out
they were almost frozen. They fed on the bears and
foxes they could trap, and made clothing out of the fur;
so great was the cold that it froze even the oil in their
clock; to keep from freezing in their sleep they heated
stones and took them into their beds. They were
afflicted, and some were killed, by scurvy. Yet they did
not lose heart: to celebrate Twelfth Night they amused
themselves choosing a king of Novaya Zemlya—the
ship's gunner—and when spring returned they loosened
their joints by playing golf.

Their ship was useless, but in June 1597 lack of food
forced them to embark in two small boats, an appalling
task in so cold a climate for men enfeebled by hunger
and disease. They met some Russians and found a grass
that overcame the scurvy; and at last, after getting
supplies of food from another Dutch vessel, they
succeeded in reaching Holland, where they had been
given up for dead. But not all of them reached home;
Barentz himself had died on the coast of Novaya
Zemlya.

Ten years later, the British explorer Henry Hudson
made a very daring venture; he would try to reach
China by sailing past the North Pole! This did not seem
so rash then as it would now, for some of the maps
indicated a possible route—across what was called the

Polar Basin, an imaginary open sea in the far north—and Barentz's report on the mild climate of Spitzbergen had been very encouraging. In 1607, taking his young son with him, Hudson made his first attempt, hoping to find a passage between Greenland and Spitzbergen, whose west coast he surveyed. Needless to say he failed; but the information he brought back was helpful to the whalers, and before the fog and ice drove him back he got further north—within 20° of the Pole—than any other explorer.

The next year he made a second attempt, this time between Spitzbergen and Novaya Zemlya. Again he failed, and he reported to the newly-formed East India Company, which had supported his ventures, that the only hope of reaching China through these waters was between Vaigach Island and the mainland of Russia. In 1609 he attempted this, and again he failed; and by 1624 the quest for a North-East Passage seemed so hopeless that even the Dutch abandoned it.

These failures led to fresh attempts to find the North-West Passage. The geographer Humphrey Gilbert, assuming that America was really Ancient Atlantis, decided that it must have some channel in the north to correspond with the Magellan Straits in the south.

The first to test this theory was Martin Frobisher, who in 1576 discovered what he called Meta Incognita ('unknown middle land') in South-East Baffin Land. To its north was what he thought was the Passage. The Eskimos whom he met astonished him; thinking they

E

had captured five of his men he kidnapped one of them, who caused much excitement in England until he caught cold and died.

Another of Frobisher's finds aroused greater excitement, for some ore he had brought with him was found to contain gold. Naturally his next voyage was made not to reach China but simply to look for wealth. Both this and his third voyage accomplished little, but Frobisher believed that if he had not been hampered by his instructions he would have got right through to the Pacific.

In 1585 and the two following years John Davis went further north than Frobisher, making three voyages between Greenland and Baffin Land. Unlike Frobisher, he was able to make friends with the Eskimos, and his men even taught them to play football. He brought home a cargo of fish and seal-skins, and though he had not discovered the North-West Passage he was certain that there was such a route, while his attempt to find it had enabled him to explore both sides of Davis Strait.

Hudson, who had failed to reach China across the Pole and north of Russia, now joined in the quest for the North-West Passage. His first attempt, in 1609, was made further to the south, and on this he discovered the Hudson River, in New York State.

On his second voyage west, in 1610, he traversed Hudson Strait and sought in vain for the Passage in Hudson Bay. His ship ran aground and was frozen in, so that he had to winter in the Bay. Food ran so short that the explorers were driven to eating moss, which they said was worse than sawdust, and frogs; the Eskimos were hostile, and the crews got unruly and threatened mutiny.

In the summer he agreed to return home, but when his ship was again stopped by the ice the crew broke into open mutiny. They thrust Hudson, his son, and the sick into a small boat, gave them a few meagre supplies, and turned them adrift. Then, except for the ship's carpenter, who at the last minute refused to desert his captain, they sailed away; with some difficulty they reached England, bringing with them Hudson's log-books and charts. But although rescue expeditions attempted to find him, nobody knows what became of that boatload of victims, treacherously abandoned in Hudson Bay.

Among the other explorers who sought for the North-West Passage was William Baffin. In 1616 he went further up Davis Strait, between Greenland and Labrador, than had hitherto been done; beyond a great sea, Baffin Bay, he discovered Jones and Lancaster Sounds. But it would be impossible, he decided, to reach China through either of these, and he was very doubtful about Hudson Bay further south. His opinion carried great weight, and as later attempts were equally unsuccessful, the quest for a trade-route to Asia round North America was given up.

15 Exploring Asia

In the seventeenth century, explorers were beginning
to give up hope of finding a practicable sea-route to
the Indies other than the perilous voyage round Cape
Horn. They now began making expeditions into the
unknown interior of Asia and America, and also in
quest of another vast unknown continent, thought to
extend far round the South Pole.

Now, too, they had better aids to navigation than
their predecessors. The Age of Discovery was also the
beginning of the Scientific Age, and this made it clear
how right Henry the Navigator had been when he got
the theoretical students to aid the seamen. Observatories, including that of Greenwich, were built for this

very purpose; and Learned Societies, including the Royal Society, were founded with the aim both of increasing knowledge and of making use of it. Expeditions were sent out not only for geographical but also for scientific discovery: in 1698 Edmond Halley, later to become Astronomer Royal, was given command of a vessel sent out to study the variations of the compass in the North Atlantic.

Working together, the 'back-room boys' and the seafarers achieved splendid results. They charted the known world more accurately than had ever been possible, and hoped to extend their charts until they covered the whole earth. They devised instruments which would enable a navigator on a ship far out at sea, or an explorer in unmapped country, to find out just where he was.

For this two things had to be known: the latitude, distance north or south of the equator; and longitude, distance east or west of their homeland.

The first was fairly easy to find. The observer had to measure the distance above the horizon of the noon sun or of the Pole Star, and he could work out the latitude from that. Some of the instruments he used were rather crude.

The cross-staff, which dates back at least to the fourteenth century, consisted of a long graduated rod with an adjustable cross-bar which could be slid along it. The observer adjusted it until, when he held the end of the staff to his eye, the horizon seemed to be at one end of the cross-bar and the star, or the lower edge of the sun, at the other. The back-staff was an improvement devised maybe two centuries later: to avoid being dazzled the observer stood with his back to the sun and observed its reflection in a small mirror which formed part of the instrument.

The astrolabe which astronomers used to study the sky was too complicated for use at sea, but possibly in the fifteenth century the simpler 'seaman's astrolabe' was produced. It consisted of a brass circle graduated after the style of a protractor, with sights to be aligned on a star and a plumb-line to show the vertical. Like cross-staff and back-staff, it was difficult to use on a wave-tossed ship.

The most practical instrument for finding the latitude was the sextant, which came into use in the eighteenth century; several Fellows of the Royal Society had a share in its invention. It was used by adjusting its mirror until the reflection of sun or star seemed to touch the horizon. It was very accurately made, and could be used on the unsteady deck of a ship.

Knowing the bearings of the port he wanted to reach, the pilot brought his ship to the same latitude; then by 'running his easting down'—steering due east or west— he was able to reach it. He judged distances by 'dead reckoning' based on his idea of the speed he was making and allowing for currents or winds. This method was clumsy and unreliable; so a method of finding the longitude was badly needed.

This could be done if local time, as shown by the sun, could be compared with time at, say, the Greenwich meridian. But when clocks were inaccurate and un-reliable, how could the observer know the Greenwich time? After the English fleet suffered heavily off the Scilly Isles, in 1707, owing, it was thought, to the pilot's not knowing his exact position, Parliament offered a reward to anyone who could devise an accurate method of finding longitude at sea.

Not for years was the reward won, and the man who gained it was neither a seaman nor a scientist but an instrument-maker. John Harrison was already noted for the accuracy of his pendulum clocks when in 1735, after six years' work, he produced the first of his chrono-meters ('time measurers'). It was a great advance on any previous timekeeper, and was remarkably accurate, while his second and third models were even better. His 'Number 4' chronometer was officially tested on a voyage to Jamaica, and at first the pilots thought it a failure, for the longitude it showed did not agree with their 'dead reckoning', and their experience made them certain they were right. But when they sighted Madeira they found that the chronometer had been far more accurate than themselves; and when they reached Jamaica, after a voyage of ten weeks, it had lost only five seconds. Thanks to Harrison and his chronometer, the problem of finding the longitude had been solved.

While new lands were being discovered in the West, the older lands of the East were also being explored. An Italian traveller, Ludovico di Varthema, travelled widely, simply because he wanted 'to behold the various kingdoms of the world'. Thinking that Egypt was well enough known already, in 1502 he entered Arabia, where he joined the escort of a caravan of pilgrims bound for the holy cities of the Mohammedans, and he helped to ward off attacks by the Arabs. He was the first European ever to visit Mecca and Medina, and to describe the ceremonies carried out by the pilgrims.

Though imprisoned in Aden, he managed to escape to Africa; then from Arabia he crossed the sea to India. After visiting Persia, he returned to India and journeyed on to Ceylon, Malaya, and the Spice Islands, where he gained much information useful to the Portuguese when they succeeded in reaching these regions by way of the Cape. Among other things, near Java he learned something remarkable, which showed that navigation was carried out in lands as yet unknown: down in the south, the captain told him, there were seafarers who steered by the Southern Cross.

Though Chancelor, when he visited Russia, had failed to find the North-East Passage, he had opened up that great country for trade. Hoping to extend this to China, the Muscovy Company in 1557 sent its agent, Anthony Jenkinson, who had taken part in Chancelor's expedition, back to Moscow. Here the Czar, Ivan the Terrible, received him kindly and gave him letters of introduction to the rulers of Asia.

Having visited Nijni Novgorod, famous for its great annual fair, Jenkinson accompanied a large Russian fleet down the Volga to Astrakhan; he was the first

Englishman ever to cross Russia from the White Sea to the Caspian and to display the Red Cross of St. George on its waters. Thence he crossed the desert eastwards to Bokhara, facing not only such natural hardships as lack of water, but also an attack by an outlaw prince. Having taken suitable gifts back to Ivan, he returned to England.

In 1562 he made a second journey down the Volga, this time hoping to open up trade with Persia. Here the Shah, a Mohammedan fanatically opposed to Christianity, threatened to behead him and send his head as a present to the Sultan of Turkey—but changed his mind when he realized that this would hardly encourage foreign trade! So Jenkinson left Persia unharmed, with rich gifts for the Czar and with silk and dye-stuffs for the Muscovy Company. Unfortunately trade across Russia with Persia was too difficult, but nonetheless he had done much to extend knowledge about both countries.

Other agents of the British trading companies reached the Far East by land or sea. They too had to face many hardships and perils, not only hunger, disease and tempest but human enemies, and not only their old enemies the Spanish and Portuguese, but also the Dutch, for they too were striving to get an increasing share in the Eastern trade. These merchant-adventurers learned much about the lands they visited—but their real aim was not discovery but trade, and there were far too many of them to mention here.

.   .   .   .   .

The Russians themselves were becoming interested in commerce and in the development of their own land. It was the aim of Peter the Great, ruler of Russia in the early-eighteenth century, to modernize his realm, to explore its vast expanse, to develop its arts and sciences, and to trade with China through the North-East Passage.

His work went on even after he died in January 1725, for a few days later one of his Danish shipbuilders, Vitus Bering, began work on a project which Peter had ordered. It was not clear how far eastwards Russia extended, and it even seemed likely that it might be joined to Western America to form one great land-mass.

With immense difficulty, and in the face of great peril, Bering crossed Siberia, then largely unknown country, to the Sea of Okhotsk. Having built a small vessel he crossed the sea to the Kamchatka Peninsula, where he made his base. He had taken three years to get there, and though there was plenty of timber available locally with which he could build his exploring vessel, the *Gabriel*, all her rigging and gear had had to be laboriously transported right across Siberia.

In 1728 he sailed north-eastwards from his base, and at last he realized that he had attained the furthermost point of Russia. Feeling that he had now accomplished his task and found a passage whereby China could be reached from the eastern part of Russia's northern coast, he turned back to Kamchatka, and charted its southern coast, which hitherto had never been surveyed. Unfortunately the mists had kept him, when he was off East Cape, from seeing that some miles to its east there began another mighty landmass.

Although Bering had spent five arduous years at the ends of the earth, he found himself blamed when he returned to civilization for not having gone further. So, in 1741, he made a second voyage beyond Russia's easternmost point; this time the weather was clear enough for him to see to eastward a chain of high snow-clad mountains. He had discovered Alaska, the most westerly part of America.

He measured the strait which separated the two continents, and began to explore the Alaskan coast. This was difficult even to approach because of the weather and of the uncharted islands along its shore and across the strait. On one of these, Bering Island, the most westerly of the Aleutians, his ship was wrecked and he and his companions had to winter. Sheltering underground from the bitter cold, short of food, and ravaged by scurvy, a number of them died, and among these was Bering himself. The survivors managed to build a ship from the wreckage and returned to Kamchatka.

Though Peter's work was continued by his successors, Russia for some time remained backward in science compared with the other countries, as a French scientist pointed out rather scathingly when he visited it in 1763. Annoyed at this, the Empress Catherine II instructed her Academy of Sciences at St. Petersburg (now Leningrad) to undertake a systematic survey of her mighty empire.

In 1768 twelve scientists, headed by the German naturalist Pierre Simon Pallas, with their assistants and equipment, began their survey. After six years of intensive work, which involved much suffering and hardship, they returned after having traversed a vaster territory, and collected more information, than had ever been done before.

There had long been a trade in ivory, but hitherto it had not been known whence it came. Now its origin was made clear, for the expedition discovered the bodies of huge creatures preserved in the snow of Northern Siberia. They resembled elephants, but were covered not with a leathery hide but with long shaggy fur. These animals, previously unknown to science, are still called by their Russian name: mammoths.

The newly-discovered Alaska seemed to give a chance of discovering the North-West Passage from its Pacific end. Among those who tried to accomplish this, in 1785, was a French nobleman, François de La Pérouse; failing, he instead explored the American coast southwards as far as the Queen Charlotte Islands. He then crossed the Pacific by way of the Hawaiian Islands, and explored the seas which separate Japan—which had now shut itself off from communication with the outside world—from Korea and Chinese Tartary. Attempting to sail northwards up the Gulf of Tartary between the mainland and Sakhalin Island, but finding the channel impassable, he then discovered the La Pérouse Strait, separating that island from another, Yezo. Having passed through the Kurile Islands he sent his records home from Kamchatka and thereby saved them, for a few years later his ships were lost exploring the Pacific Islands, and he and his companions were either drowned or slaughtered by the natives.

16 Unknown Southern Land

THOUGH Ptolemy had plainly been wrong in believing that China and Africa were joined to a great southern landmass, many people still believed that there was a great undiscovered continent far in the south: it seemed necessary to balance the huge landmasses of the north. It had even been given a name: *Terra Australis Incognita*, 'The Unknown Southern Land', and, of course, it was supposed to be fabulously rich.

There were rumours that this land had actually been sighted. Magellan had fancied that Tierra del Fuego, the 'land of fires' south of the Magellan Straits, was one of its peninsulas. Drake disproved this theory by showing that the Tierra is actually a group of islands, but that did not prove that the undiscovered continent was unreal. And when seamen reported that south of Java there were people who steered by the Southern Cross, they suggested that the Unknown Southern Land not merely existed, but that it was actually inhabited.

Drake may have hoped to sight this land during his voyage round the world, but the first serious attempt to find it was made in 1605 by two Spanish explorers, Pedros de Quiros and Luiz de Torres. They thought they had succeeded when, after discovering a number of island groups, they came to a larger landmass; but after Quiros had sailed away, Torres found that it was only another island, Santo in the New Hebrides.

Steering north-north-west, Torres reached New Guinea, and sailed past its southern coast, thereby showing that it was an island. What he did not realize was that he was then traversing a channel, the Torres Strait, and that, a little to his south, what looked like distant islands were really the mountains of a continent hitherto unknown. In the same year the Dutch seaman William Janszoon was the first to sight and land on that very continent; he did not realize what it was, and merely thought it was part of New Guinea.

Several other landings were made on this continent, part of which was called New Holland, but as yet nobody suspected its extent. To ascertain whether these landfalls proved the existence of the Unknown Southern Land or not, and also to explore the southern part of the Indian Ocean, Abel Tasman sailed from Java in 1642. After visiting Mauritius he steered southwards and then, at about 50° south, eastwards. This course brought him to an unknown coast, which he called Van Dieman's Land, but the natives were too hostile for him to explore it.

After sailing round its southern coast, he cruised on eastward, and reached another unknown shore; he called this Staten Land. As he coasted it northwards he came to an immense bay, but the tides and the weather kept him from penetrating far into it, and when he landed on its shore some of his men were killed in a skirmish with the fierce natives. Beyond the bay the land continued northwards, and he went on coasting it; then he returned to Java, convinced that he had at last found the Unknown Southern Land.

The first of the two countries he had discovered is now called Tasmania, and the second New Zealand. He had also discovered the Tonga Islands and other island groups. Moreover, without realizing this and without seeing any part of it except the island of Tasmania, in the course of his voyage he had cruised round Australia.

The Dutch did not follow up Tasman's discoveries, and the next explorations of the Southern Pacific were made by the British. Some indeed were made by the buccaneers.

One of these adventurers, William Dampier, set out in 1686 on a buccaneering expedition. From Guam in the East Indies he sailed for the Spice Islands, but instead he reached a coast which he realized must belong to New Holland: he could not be sure if it were an island or part of a continent, though he was certain it was joined neither to Asia, Africa, nor America, and that it must be very large. But far from being fabulously rich, it was poverty-stricken. Its inhabitants, he said, were the 'miserablest people in the world', ugly, indolent, without any houses, very scantily clad, and living on 'a small sort of fish' grilled over the coals.

This exploit earned him command of an expedition sent out in 1699, its object being to study New Holland

—its geography, its inhabitants, and its minerals. Dampier had meant, as before, to approach it from the east, but a change in his plans brought him to Sharks Bay on its west coast. Surveying its shores north-east-ward, he discovered the Dampier Archipelago; then a shortage of water and an outbreak of scurvy drove him to New Guinea. He traversed the Dampier Straits to its north-east, and so reached another unknown island, which he called New Britain. But his ship was now un-seaworthy, and though he had had her repaired in Java, she went down off Ascension Island, taking with her many of his records.

Enough survived of Dampier's records to show that he was a keen observer. He was the first to describe a typhoon, and to mention animals previously unheard of, the kangaroos. With better training he might have become a brilliant naturalist, one of those thinkers whose work is so essential in exploration.

In 1769 a transit of Venus across the face of the sun was forecast, and this would enable the distance of the sun to be calculated more accurately. It would be favourably visible from the South Seas; so, with government support, the Royal Society sent out an expedition to observe it.

The Commander they appointed, James Cook, had special qualifications for the work. He was a brave and skilful seaman, having taken part in the amphibious operation by which Wolfe captured Quebec. He had charted and surveyed the coasts of the St. Lawrence and of Newfoundland; and he was himself competent in astronomy, having observed and reported on an eclipse of the sun. He was accompanied by Joseph Banks, one of Britain's leading naturalists, thanks to whose generosity H.M.S. *Endeavour* was specially equipped with an excellent library and scientific apparatus; she had on board two painters and draughtsmen.

Though the ostensible purpose of the expedition was scientific, Cook had further instructions. He was to 'make discovery' of the rumoured southern continent, and failing this he was to visit New Zealand and explore as much as possible of its coast. Plainly the idea was to annex and colonize these distant lands.

Sailing in 1768, the *Endeavour* rounded Cape Horn, and soon Banks was eagerly botanizing on the Pacific islands. Tahiti was reached in April, the scientific equipment landed, and the transit of Venus observed in splendid conditions. Much information was also collected about Tahiti and the rest of the Society Islands.

This scientific work satisfactorily accomplished, Cook now proceeded with his other task by visiting New Zealand. This aroused much lively discussion, most of the expedition believing that the Unknown Southern Land had at last been reached. It now had to be explored; by cruising round it, Cook discovered that part at any rate of New Zealand—North Island—was separated from whatever lands lay to its south by that great inlet which Tasman had mistaken for a bay and which was now found to be a strait.

It still seemed as if the land south of this strait might be part of the Unknown Continent, but Cook disproved this by sailing round South Island. Having taken possession of both islands for Britain, he decided to return home not eastwards by the storm-swept Cape Horn, but westwards round the Cape of Good Hope.

This route brought him to an unknown landmass far too great to be an island. It could not possibly be part of the Unknown Southern Land, for to its south lay the sea, and he was not certain whether or not it was connected with Van Dieman's Land. He coasted it northwards, made several landings, and annexed it for Britain under the name of New South Wales. Near one inlet grew so great a variety of flowers that Banks delightedly called it Botany Bay.

One night the explorers were peacefully sailing north-wards when suddenly they were aroused by a terrific shock: the *Endeavour* had struck a sunken rock—and it was coral, which because of its sharp points and rough surface is especially destructive. For two days she was held fast, but a high tide enabled the crew to free her: when she was beached for repairs it was found that a piece of coral had snapped off and plugged the rent in her hull. In this painful way Cook discovered the Great Barrier Reef, whose existence he could not have sus-pected, for it is like nothing else in the world.

To get clear of the Reef, which extends almost down the east coast of Australia, was difficult, and it was difficult, too, to traverse the Torres Straits, with their many small reefs and islets. The *Endeavour* had to seek refuge in Batavia for necessary repairs. This was unfortunate, for the unhealthy climate wrought havoc among the crew, who hitherto had been almost free from disease. Then, after calling at Cape Town, the ship reached home, bringing the magnificent botanical collection made by Banks.

This achievement led to Cook's being sent with two vessels to seek for further undiscovered lands in the South Seas. Captain Cook, as he now was, sailed southwards past the Cape of Good Hope, and though hindered by masses of floating ice he managed in 1773 to cross the Antarctic Circle—the first explorer ever to do this. Prevented by the ice from going further south, he sailed to New Zealand and spent some time cruising to its south and east; again he crossed the Antarctic Circle, going further south than before, to 71°. Having returned to New Zealand and discovered some more islands, he sailed for home round Cape Horn. Thus he had circumnavigated the earth in southern waters without finding any trace north of the Antarctic Circle of the Unknown Southern Land.

This question having been settled, his third voyage, begun in 1776, had a very different aim, to seek for the North-West Passage by coasting Alaska—though, as before, he was also to annex any unknown lands he might reach. Having made some minor discoveries, and shown that some 'discoveries' claimed by other explorers were baseless, he made a careful but fruitless search of the north-west coast of America for any channel which might lead to the Atlantic. He sailed between Asia and Alaska, and as far as the ice would allow he made his way along the northern shores of both. He gave their names to Bering Straits and to the two headlands between which they are narrowest, Prince of Wales Cape (in Alaska) and East Cape, as well as to the limits of his exploration beyond the Straits, Icy Cape to the east and North Cape to the west.

When the onset of winter drove him southwards he revisited the Sandwich Islands, which he had discovered earlier on his journey. And here, in 1779, he was killed in a dispute with the natives.

Cook had claimed for Britain Australia, New Zealand, and very many islands. He had shown that the Unknown Southern Land, though so long believed in, did not really exist, at any rate in the temperate regions. That there might be some such continent nearer to the Pole he did not deny; in fact, he thought that there was and that he had caught a distant glimpse of its snow-clad mountains across the ice-fields. But if so, it lay in regions far too cold to be habitable.

Even more important, perhaps, he had shown how a ship's company could be kept in good health and immune from scurvy, by a well-balanced diet, including fresh foods and lemon and orange juice, and by strict attention to cleanliness.

17 Inland into America

EXPLORATION and development in North America were slower than in the rest of the continent. As early as 1584 Walter Raleigh had tried to found a colony in Virginia, but he had failed, and it was not until 1606 that the colony was established. One of its pioneers was Captain John Smith. When he was captured by a Red Indian tribe, the chief's daughter, Pocahontas, pleaded for him, and his friendship with the Indians induced them to trade with the emigrants, so saving the little colony from starvation.

Smith later explored a more northerly region which he called New England. Though Bartholomew Gosnold had already visited it in 1602 and discovered

Cape Cod, its chief colony, Massachusetts, was not successfully established until 1620, when the Pilgrim Fathers arrived in the *Mayflower*.

The restoration of Charles II in 1660 led to the founding of several 'plantations', as they were then called, on the North American coast. By 1760 the whole of this, from Maine to Georgia, was British. The settlements did not extend far inland, partly because the Indians were hostile, and partly because the Blue Ridge and Alleghany Mountains were difficult to cross. Routes across them were found by such explorers as Daniel Boone, who in 1767 reached the Blue Grass region of Kentucky: some of them were looking for gold, some for furs, some for trade with the Indians, and some for a route to Asia.

Though it was nearly fifty years before the French followed up Cartier's discovery of Canada, they then made far more rapid progress than the English further south. They got on better with the Indians, and moreover the St. Lawrence enabled them to penetrate far inland. After founding Quebec and Montreal, Samuel de Champlain reached the Great Lakes in 1615; in 1634 he organized an exploring expedition to seek for a route to the Pacific. Beyond Lake Michigan its leader, Jean Nicollet, reached the divide between the St. Lawrence and what the Indians called the Mississippi ('Great River'); naturally he thought that this must flow into the Pacific.

Other French explorers, foremost of whom were the Jesuit missionaries, traversed the region around the

Great Lakes. Soon it was realized that the Mississippi flowed not eastwards, but southwards, and in 1681 Rene la Salle followed it to the sea. Arriving at the Gulf of Mexico, he claimed the whole river-valley in the name of King Louis of France, calling it Louisiana.

This river, like the St. Lawrence and the Great Lakes, enabled the French to penetrate still further into North America. South of their flourishing colony in Canada they extended a line of forts; this alarmed the British colonists, who felt that they were being hemmed in between the French and the sea and were in danger of being overrun.

To the west Spanish explorers from Mexico were making their way northwards. Some were traders seeking for gold, precious stones, or fur, while others were Jesuit missionaries seeking to convert the Indians. Inland they reached the Great Salt Lake of Utah, but here the country is so arid that the Spaniards did not follow up this discovery, preferring to develop Texas to its east and California to its west. So far north did they travel that at last they reached the coast which Drake had claimed for England under the name of New Albion. When in 1789 they seized an important trading post which Cook had established at Nootka Sound, a war between Britain and Spain seemed likely.

Neither country really wanted war, however, so in 1791 the British Government sent George Vancouver, who had sailed with Cook, to try to settle the dispute and also to seek for the North-West Passage and explore the coast. Having made some discoveries on the southern coast of New Holland and elsewhere in the Pacific, Vancouver made friendly contact with the Spaniards at Nootka Sound. He failed to find the North-West Passage, and reported to the Admiralty that it did not exist, but in seeking for it he made a detailed survey of a long stretch of the American coast.

He moreover reached a satisfactory arrangement with the Spaniards, who agreed that the British should have trading and colonizing rights in the North Pacific. This showed that in spite of the Pope's decree they no longer claimed the whole of the western coast of America.

Since the time of Charles II the English Hudson's Bay Company had been trading in furs and minerals. It began to explore the country west of Hudson Bay; and in 1769 Samuel Hearne set out in quest of some rich copper-mines reported by the Indians. He discovered the Coppermine River and followed it to its mouth in the Arctic, and when returning overland he also discovered the Great Slave Lake. His explorations showed clearly, however, that there was no North-West Passage opening from Hudson Bay.

From the Great Slave Lake a river flowed westwards; if it reached the Pacific it might become a useful trade-route, so in 1789 Alexander Mackenzie decided to find out by following it to the sea. Even to reach the lake needed several portages, crossing it was difficult because of the ice, while on the journey down-stream food ran short. In spite of such setbacks, Mackenzie at last sighted the sea—and found it was not the Pacific, but the Arctic. Having settled this question, he returned, completing a journey of nearly three thousand miles through the bleak north-west territories of Canada, in little more than a hundred days.

In 1792 he began another adventurous journey through the unexplored country. Starting from Atha-baska Lake, he followed the Peace River to its source in the Rocky Mountains. Then came a laborious and difficult portage of his equipment through the bush on the mountain-slopes, where one false step might lead to a headlong drop into the water. Though his Indian guides were untrustworthy and his men unruly, Mackenzie persuaded them to continue across the crest of the Rockies.

He then embarked down the Fraser River, but as this became unnavigable he had to make another portage across a divide to the Bellacoola River, which brought him to the Pacific coast just too late to meet Vancouver's expedition. Mackenzie was the first explorer to cross these northern regions from sea to sea, and his work later enabled much of their western part to be settled. Thanks largely to such explorations, Canada became the flourishing dominion it is today.

Wolfe's victory at Quebec in 1759 not only brought Canada under British rule, though it still left France in possession of Louisiana; it also freed the older British colonies from the threat of French domination. Some long-smouldering grievances against Britain now came to a head, and in 1776 the Declaration of Independence converted the former 'plantations' into the first thirteen of the United States.

Soon the newly-formed Union was enabled to more than double its territory, for in 1803, by the Louisiana Purchase, Napoleon sold it the whole Mississippi Valley. Naturally this vast region had to be surveyed, especially as its boundaries were uncertain, so Meriwether Lewis and William Clark were sent to explore the Missouri River and its tributaries, and if possible to reach the Pacific.

Having wintered with the Red Indians of Dakota, they crossed the Rockies and followed the Columbia River down to the sea. Forced to return by shortage of supplies, they separated for a time, Clark following the Yellowstone River before rejoining Lewis on the Missouri. Between them they travelled over seven thousand miles, and in addition to exploring a vast area and finding a route to the Pacific they enabled a region which might otherwise have formed part of Canada to become, in recent times, the States of Oregon and Washington.

Further to the south, another area was explored from 1841 to 1854 by John Charles Frémont, whose guide was one of the great American backwoodsmen and 'scouts', Kit Carson. Frémont surveyed the country between the Columbia River and California; here, as in Canada, the work of such explorers opened up the West for settlement and it made possible the growth of the modern United States.

The extreme north-west of America is so bleak that development was slow both in the Yukon, a Canadian Territory, and in Alaska, which the Russians had sold to the United States. Suddenly, however, the discovery of rich deposits of gold in the Klondike led to the famous Gold Rush of 1896 and to the systematic surveying of both regions.

So vast is South America, so difficult to traverse are its forests, and so fierce are some of its tribes, that in the early nineteenth century much of it was still unexplored; because of political troubles, little was known even about Mexico. Both regions, as well as Cuba, were systematically studied from 1799 to 1803 by Alexander von Humboldt, one of the greatest of scientific explorers, and renowned for the advances he made in many branches of knowledge.

In South America Humboldt investigated the structure of the Andes Mountains and explored a number of river-basins such as the Magdalena, the Orinoco, and the Amazon. Among his achievements, he found something unique among the world's river-systems; the headwaters of the Orinoco and the Amazon are actually linked by a broad channel, the Cassiquiare, about one hundred and eighty miles long. This and his other discoveries led to further scientific explorations of South America, and these to its development.

Among these scientific explorations, one of the most important was led by Robert Fitzroy. Having spent four years in surveying the coast from the Plate River round Cape Horn to Chiloé, in 1831 he returned in the *Beagle*. With him, as naturalist to the expedition, came Charles Darwin, whose studies did for the south of the continent what Humboldt had done for its north. The *Beagle* also circumnavigated the world, and observations made during this exploration enabled Captain Fitzroy, who was a meteorologist, to compile his well-known Storm Warnings, and Darwin, who was a biologist, to arrive at his Theory of Evolution.

Not yet, however, is the South American continent completely explored, and strange rumours are still current about the mysteries hidden in its interior. In 1925 Colonel Fawcett ventured into the Mato Grasso, a dangerous region south of the Amazon, where a civilized people were supposed to live; these, he thought, might be descended from the inhabitants of Ancient Atlantis. He and his companions were never seen again. Though a rescue expedition decided that they must have been slain by the natives, it is not known for certain what became of them.

18 Into Darkest Africa

FOR a long time Africa was more completely unknown even than recently-discovered America. Apart from Egypt and the regions nearby, some stretches along the coast and up the river-mouths, and an area north of the Cape of Good Hope, it was almost completely unexplored. Its unhealthy climate, its trackless jungles, its great deserts, its fierce native tribes, and its fanatical Moslems all combined to bar the white man out.

In 1788 the African Association was formed to explore the continent and open it up for British trade and influence. The first problem to solve was that of the River Niger; little was known of this, but it was thought to flow westwards and reach the sea by such mouths as the Senegal and the Gambia. The first three attempts to explore it having failed, a fourth was made in 1795 by Mungo Park.

Some distance up the Gambia he journeyed over land and crossed the Senegal. Though robbed of all his possessions, imprisoned, pursued by armed bandits, and nearly killed by fever and thirst, he at last reached the Niger. And, as he had half expected, it flowed not westwards towards the coast but inland towards the east.

In 1805 he led an expedition too large to be efficient, and, moreover, badly organized. Only a handful of survivors accompanied him to the Niger, where they built a boat to sail downstream; they had got as far as Bussa in Nigeria when they too perished.

Another attempt to reach the Niger was made across the Sahara in 1823 when Denham, Clapperton, and Oudney journeyed almost due south from Tripoli. Their route brought them to Lake Chad; but they realized that this, though a great discovery, could not be the course of the river, which in fact flowed much further west.

While Denham explored the country round the lake, his companions turned westwards towards Kano, a great Mohammedan trading centre. Oudney died during the journey; though himself ill, Clapperton managed to reach Sokoto, but he could not get permission to visit the Niger. Instead he returned towards the Lake, arriving so worn down by fever that Denham could scarcely recognize him.

In 1825 Clapperton at last reached the Niger, this time by landing at Lagos and approaching it from the south. At Bussa he learned how Mungo Park and his companions had been killed, their boat swamped in the treacherous rapids. Though Clapperton himself died at Sokoto, his companion, Richard Lander, managed to get back to the coast.

In 1830 Lander, accompanied by his brother John, again reached Bussa from the coast, and by paddling downstream they came to the river-mouth. Thus the problem of the Niger was solved: rising near the west coast, it follows a long curving course inland, reaching the sea in the Gulf of Benin. For this achievement Lander was honoured by the Royal Geographical Society. Formed in 1830, this society had not only taken over the work of the African Association, but in addition aimed at advancing knowledge, by exploration and study, of the whole earth.

As elsewhere, the aim of other explorers was to take Christianity into 'darkest Africa'. The missionaries in Bechuanaland were joined, in 1841, by David Livingstone, not only a minister but also a doctor and a student of science. Hardly had he arrived when he travelled alone into the unknown country further north so as to learn the language and customs of the natives. Soon he had won their friendship and was doing splendid work among them, but this was interrupted by the Boers, who were trekking northwards and driving the negroes into the desert.

Somewhere beyond the desert was rumoured to be a great lake near which the unfortunate refugees would find a welcome, and in 1849 Livingstone went to seek for it. In spite of lack of water and other difficulties, he and two white hunters at last crossed the Kalahari Desert and discovered Lake Ngami. Two years later he made another important discovery, that the River Zambesi flows right through the heart of Africa— formerly it was thought to rise much further east.

Returning into South Africa, he found that here the

Boers were making missionary work almost impossible. He hoped to carry it on further north, but he realized that first the region would have to be systematically explored. Having been trained in such work and acquired the necessary scientific instruments, he again crossed the Kalahari to the Zambesi.

Here his exploration really began. Following the river westwards, he crossed the divide into the Congo Basin and pushed on towards the sea. He ran short of food; some of the tribes were hostile; his native followers lost their nerve and threatened to forsake him, and he himself became so weak he could hardly walk unaided. Yet he at last reached Loanda on the coast.

Hardly had he regained his strength when he began the return journey eastwards. Again he had to face danger and difficulty, and again his health failed, but he succeeded in taking his native followers back to their homeland.

He did not stop here, but followed the Zambesi eastwards, on his way discovering the Victoria Falls. Again hostile tribes threatened his life, but his cool courage and friendliness overcame them, and he reached the mouth of the river in Portuguese East Africa.

When, after an absence of sixteen years, he returned to England he had explored vast regions hitherto unknown; he had made important discoveries, including Lake Ngami and the Victoria Falls; he had traced the course of the Zambesi from its headwaters to the sea. He had made clear the structure of Central Africa, which consists of a vast tableland somewhat depressed

F

at its centre and with gaps in its rim through which the great rivers reach the sea. He had opened the country up not only for trade but for Christianity. He was honoured both as an explorer and as a missionary. Yet his one wish was to get back to his work.

The great African mystery, far greater than that of the Niger, was the source of the Nile, and the cause of its strange annual flooding at the right time to grow corn. Geographers had long puzzled over this; Ptolemy had heard that it rises in two great lakes in the heart of Africa, fed by melting snow from a range called 'The Mountains of the Moon'.

In 1613 Pedro Paez solved the problem of its annual flooding. Its main stream, the White Nile, is fed by its tributary the Blue Nile, which is swollen every year by rainfall from the mountains of Abyssinia. Paez also discovered the source of the Blue Nile, near Lake Tseana, but little more was known of this until James Bruce studied it in 1768.

Still, however, the source of the White Nile remained a mystery: somewhere in Central Africa was supposed to be a huge lake from which it flowed. In 1856 an experienced traveller, Richard Burton, volunteered to seek for this lake. The Royal Geographical Society accepted his offer, and with him went John Speke. From Zanzibar the two, with great difficulty, crossed a stretch of unhealthy country to Lake Tanganyika. This, they thought, must surely be the source of the Nile—until they heard of another great lake somewhere to its north.

Burton's health broke down; but Speke, though nearly blinded by sun-glare and partially deaf, reached a lake even larger than Tanganyika. Its native name was Nyanza, but he called it Victoria; this, he felt, must be the Nile's true source.

This was not certain, however, so in 1860, with J. A. Grant, he again visited Lake Victoria. Here they learned of another lake further upstream, but the natives kept them from reaching it.

Instead, they passed on their information to another explorer, Samuel Baker, who with his wife was also seeking for the source of the Nile. In spite of fever and sunstroke, of desertion by their porters, and of shortage of food, the Bakers at length reached this upper lake. Regarding it as one, at least, of the sources of the Nile, Baker called it Albert Nyanza.

In 1858 Livingstone had returned to East Africa as British Consul; he was heading a large expedition and was trying to organize an important mission. But he always worked best independently; in his small steam-launch he cruised up the Zambesi seeking for a large lake of which the natives spoke. Forced by the rapids to travel overland, after a difficult journey he discovered Lake Shirwa in 1859. Beyond this he reached another larger lake which was already known but which had never been fully explored, Nyasa.

Later he tried to reach this lake direct from the coast, up the Rovuma River. Finding this impossible, he re-visited it from the south and explored the country to

its west. When recalled by the British Government he
realized that his steam-launch might fall into the hands
of the slave-traders, so he daringly steered it across the
Indian Ocean to Bombay.

When he returned to Africa in 1866, he aimed at
combining his missionary work with an attempt to solve
that age-old problem, the source of the Nile; he thought
this as important as the North-West Passage. Journeying up the Rovuma and then across country to Lake
Nyasa and pressing on westwards, he encountered endless difficulty. His native bearers were troublesome; the
tribes he encountered were at war; worst of all, he was
ageing and his health failing. When his medicine-chest
was stolen, he felt as if it were a death-blow.

Yet, almost too weak to keep up with his men, he
pressed doggedly on. He reached Lake Liemba; this
was not an actual discovery, for it is the southern part
of Lake Tanganyika, but his work made it more
accurately known. After a brief rest on its shores, he discovered two more lakes, Mweru and Bangweolo.

Returning, almost worn out, to Lake Tanganyika,
Livingstone was surprised to meet Henry Morton
Stanley, a journalist whom a New York paper had sent
out to look for him. Together they explored the northern
part of the Lake and proved that it could not be the
source of the Nile. After Stanley left him, Livingstone,
now well equipped and partially restored to health,
continued his journeys alone. Though he was finding
the Nile problem continually more difficult, he thought
the river might rise somewhere near Bangweolo. But

once more his powers failed, and he was still vainly looking for its source when he died in 1873.

His work was continued by Stanley who, inspired by his example, had given up journalism and become an explorer. Stanley's greatest feat was to cruise down the Congo, through regions into which even Livingstone had been unable to penetrate, to the sea. He also cleared up the Nile problem by showing that the White Nile has two separate sources. Its main source is the Victoria Nyanza, the other including not only the Albert Nyanza but another lake which he discovered, the Edward.

Thus both Speke and Baker had been right. So, for that matter, had Ptolemy, for Stanley also found that the Ruwenzori range, rising twenty thousand feet high, between Lakes Edward and Albert, is actually called by the natives 'The Mountains of the Moon'.

Much of Africa was soon colonized by the European powers. Now many of its regions have achieved self-government and others are seeking it. That it is no longer, as of old, the 'Dark Continent', is largely due to the work of missionary and other explorers, of whom the greatest was David Livingstone.

19 Known Southern Lands

Cook had annexed New Holland for Britain, but for some time his government made no use of it. Then, at the suggestion of his friend Joseph Banks, they tried to settle it with refugees, British loyalists exiled from the newly-formed United States. This scheme failed, and even when a small colony was established at Sydney it developed but slowly.

One difficulty was that, apart from the east coast which Cook had surveyed, very little was known about New Holland. It was not clear whether Tasmania formed part of it or was an island—or indeed whether the mainland itself might not be divided into two by a strait running northwards to the Gulf of Carpentaria.

Both these problems were solved by Matthew Flinders. In 1798, by sailing with George Bass through Bass Straits, he showed that Tasmania is an island and surveyed its entire coast. In 1802, by cruising right along the south coast of New Holland, he proved that this consists of one large landmass. At his suggestion it was given a new name: Australia, from the Latin word for 'southern'.

During the cruise he met a French scientific expedition. Its leader, Nicholas Baudin, hoped to annex part of the continent for France under the name of Terre Napoleon. But when at Sydney he asked how much of it was claimed by Britain, he had his answer: not only Tasmania but the whole of Australia.

Next year Flinders circumnavigated Australia, but his vessel was wrecked off Queensland. To get a rescue ship from Sydney he had to make a perilous journey, in an open boat, of two hundred and fifty leagues. When, later, he had to put in at Mauritius during the Napoleonic Wars, he was interned by the French under conditions that ruined his health and led to his early death.

Only the coast of Australia had been explored. Inland of Sydney, the Blue Mountains formed a barrier difficult to cross. So little was known about the continent, indeed, that it was thought to contain a large central sea. At last, however, in 1813, a severe drought induced G. Blaxland to look for pasture beyond the mountains. Having succeeded in crossing them he reached a country so well watered that here the town of Bathurst was founded in 1815.

Several other expeditions crossed the Blue Mountains, the most important being those led by Charles Sturt. In 1828, after travelling north-west for some months, he was delighted to come to a broad river, the Darling, abounding in wildfowl, but on reaching it he found to his horror—for the expedition was suffering from thirst —that its waters were salt: there were brine springs in its bed. Lack of fresh water forced him to return to Sydney.

In 1829 he headed another expedition, this time provided with a boat. Travelling inland south of his previous route, he reached the Murrumbidgee River. When he embarked on it, a dangerous current swept him downstream at headlong speed. After a week's cruise he emerged into a much larger river, the Murray.

This carried him into a crowd of natives, who suddenly appeared on its banks, shouting frantically and making threatening gestures. A disastrous conflict seemed probable; but suddenly the Blackfellows changed their minds and thronged peacefully round the explorers.

Further down, the river was joined by another large stream; this, Sturt realized, must be the Darling. After exploring it for a short distance he returned to the Murray, which brought him to a large lake almost at the edge of the sea. Though the lake was too shallow to be navigable, the explorers reached the coast on foot. Then they had to row back up the Murray against wind and current to the Murrumbidgee, short of food and threatened by the natives. Only after much hardship and difficulty did they succeed in reaching Sydney.

Sturt's exploration of the river-systems of New South Wales had two important results. It enabled the settlers in the Sydney region to move much further inland, and it led to the development, near the mouth of the Murray, of Adelaide.

It was from Adelaide that, in 1844, Sturt tried to cross Australia from south to north. Having first travelled up the Murray and completed the exploration of the Darling, he pushed cn further inland. His studies of bird migration had led him to expect the interior of the continent to be fertile, but instead he found himself in what he called the Great Stony Desert, as desolate and difficult to cross, he thought, as the ice-fields round the Pole. Though he reached a small lagoon in its heart, he could go no further, and it was only after very great hardships that he and his companions made their way back to civilization.

The next attempt to cross the continent was made in 1860 by Burke and Wills. Starting at Melbourne, and taking camels for traversing the desert, they reached Cooper's Creek, an inland river discovered by Sturt. Here, having made their depôt and left a rear-party, the leaders with two companions pressed on northwards. After an arduous journey they reached a tidal estuary, though they did not actually get within sight of the Gulf of Carpentaria.

The return march was far worse. One of the four died; and when the three survivors at last staggered back to Cooper's Creek they found that only a few hours before the reserve party had given them up and left, together with all the camels and horses. Exhausted and half-starved, they tried to reach Adelaide, but first Wills and then Burke perished from hunger and thirst. Their companion, King, survived only through the help the natives gave him, and by the time he was rescued he was 'wasted to a shadow'.

Undiscouraged by this tragedy, J. M. Stuart attempted a little later to cross the continent from Adelaide, following a route further west than Cooper's Creek. His first journey brought him to the centre of Australia, but the hostility of the natives drove him back. On his second he got a little further, but was baffled by lack of food and water. Only on his third attempt, in 1862, did he reach Port Darwin on Australia's north coast.

Though Western Australia had been the original New Holland, and had been discovered by Dampier before Cook was born, it was much later in being developed than the rest of the continent. Not until the French were thought to have designs on it was its first colony founded, in 1826, at King George Sound; a few years later the Swan River was explored and Perth founded. Other explorations followed, and a series of several long and hazardous journeys linked these western settlements with the rest of the continent.

Of all the early explorers of Australia, Banks had been the only one to see its great possibilities. He was right: for though until recent times the continent was inhabited solely by backward natives, it is now as civilized as any place in the world, with vast farms and flourishing industries. Its heart is a desert, but the Gold Rush of 1851 led to the development even of this.

New Zealand, too, long went unexplored, except that Stewart Island and some smaller islands to its south were accidentally discovered by whalers. The exploration of North Island was begun in 1814 by Samuel Marsden, a missionary from New South Wales. Travelling southwards from North Cape, he went beyond the Hauraki Gulf and founded a settlement at Rangihihoura.

In 1839 the recently-formed New Zealand Company chose for its first colony a site on the south of North Island which has now become Wellington. Especially important were the discoveries made by J. C. Bidwill, including Lakes Rotoaira and Taupo and the famous Hot Springs. Bidwill also climbed the volcano of Tongariro, in great danger not only from its crater but also from the Maoris, who regarded the mountain as sacred.

The Maoris, who were much more advanced and warlike than the Australian Aborigines, were for long a great obstacle to the exploration and settlement of New Zealand. At last, however, they were reconciled to the white newcomers, and the peaceful development of both islands could proceed.

South Island, which is exposed to more wintry conditions than North Island, was naturally slower in being developed, although the Gold Rush of 1861 attracted a large number of immigrants. Indeed, some parts of its south-western region are not very well known now, though otherwise both islands have been extensively explored.

New Guinea is another land which though discovered hundreds of years ago was little explored until last century. Its shape was not clearly realized until J. Moresby surveyed it in 1873; its central range of mountains was discovered only in 1896, when William MacGregor crossed the island from coast to coast. Even now, like some other regions in the East Indies, parts of the island remain to be properly explored.

20 To the North Pole

DURING THE nineteenth century explorers were
spurred on by a new motive. Expeditions were now
sent out not only to annex or colonize newly-discovered
land, to develop trade or advance science, but simply
for national prestige. Even though a place might be
very difficult to reach, uninhabitable, with no useful
minerals, and with little scientific interest, a nation
thought it a great triumph to plant its flag there.

The end of the Napoleonic Wars found many experienced naval officers unwilling to settle down to every-
day life. The idea of exploration attracted them, and
for the British the most obvious quest was the search,
through Canadian waters, for the North-West Passage.

They were much encouraged when seafarers in those waters reported that the ice-barrier seemed to be loosening, and when Sir John Barrow, Secretary to the Admiralty, offered a generous reward for the discovery of the Passage. This was now sought not as a possible trade-route but for science and geography, and as a patriotic duty, and it was sought systematically, each explorer striving to investigate some channel never yet traversed.

The first attempt to find the North-West Passage for such reasons was made in 1818 by John Ross and W. E. Parry. The expedition reached Lancaster Sound, but here Ross decided that further progress was impossible and turned back.

Many of his officers disagreed with him, and among these was Parry. In 1819 he took his two ships not only into but beyond Lancaster Sound and through Barrow Strait to Melville Island. Here they had to winter; Parry fought against scurvy by growing mustard and cress near the cabin stove-pipe, and kept his men in good spirits by amateur theatricals and by their own paper, the *North Georgian Gazette*. In the summer, before returning to Britain, he explored the island with land-parties.

Thinking that Barrow Strait was after all unlikely to lead to the Passage, Parry sought a route further south. In 1821 he explored the land north-west of Hudson Bay. After wintering here, he went northwards through Fox Channel and discovered the narrow waterway between Baffin Island and the Canadian mainland; this he named, after his ships, the Fury and Hecla Strait. Having again wintered in the ice he returned home.

In 1824 he made a third voyage, hoping to find a passage north of Baffin Island and down Prince Regent Inlet. Though he returned safely, he accomplished little, for conditions were adverse and the *Fury* became a wreck.

While Parry was on his second voyage, John Franklin was making an even more hazardous journey, leading an expedition overland through Canada from Hudson Bay to Lake Athabasca. He hoped before winter to reach the Coppermine River, but a number of hindrances, including clouds of vicious mosquitoes, delayed him. While wintering at Fort Enterprise the expedition was threatened by starvation, and was saved only by the heroism of George Back. Travelling about eighteen miles a day on snow-shoes, short of food and through intense cold, Back made the double journey of over one thousand miles to and from Lake Athabasca to get help.

It was when they reached the mouth of the Coppermine that the expedition's real task began, to explore the waters north of Canada. So irregular was the coast of Coronation Gulf that they had to paddle over five hundred miles to cover the 175 miles to Turnagain Point. Some of them reached civilization overland, after sufferings so terrible that descriptions of them appalled even hardened explorers such as Parry.

Undiscouraged by their hardships, in 1825 Franklin, with Back and another of his old comrades, John Richardson, again explored the Canadian coast. While his main party wintered at Great Bear Lake, Franklin made a preliminary journey down the Mackenzie River so as to help the expedition, next spring, to descend the river to its mouth.

Here the expedition split. Franklin travelled westwards towards Icy Cape. At Return Point the weather forced him to retreat—not realizing that another expedition, under Captain Beechey, had already doubled the Cape, and was waiting for him only a hundred miles further on.

Meanwhile Richardson had travelled eastwards towards the Coppermine River mouth. He discovered Wollaston Land, and though one of his boats was almost crushed by the ice he returned safely to Great Bear Lake, arriving a little in advance of Franklin. Reunited, the expedition again wintered on the Lake; in all, it had surveyed about a thousand miles of coast.

Explorers were now visiting the Arctic almost every year. Ross, on his second attempt to find the North-West Passage in 1829, had particularly good hopes of success, for he was the first to use a steamship in such a venture. Though his engines soon broke down, he carried on under sail, up Lancaster Sound and through Prince Regent Inlet. Thus he discovered Boothia Land, the northernmost peninsula of Canada.

Users of the compass had always known that it does not point due north. Having calculated the exact position towards which it does point, Ross made a sledge journey across heavy snow into Boothia Land towards it. It was, however, his nephew James Ross who reached the North Magnetic Pole and claimed it for Britain by building a cairn and raising the Union Flag above it.

So adverse was the weather that the explorers' ship was irretrievably frozen in. Leaving her with her colours nailed to the mast, they crossed the ice to the shore, having first replenished their stores from the wreck of Parry's *Fury*. Not until they had spent four winters in the Arctic were they rescued, half-starved and suffering badly from scurvy, by a whaler.

In 1845 Franklin, though nearly sixty, decided to make another attempt to find the North-West Passage. With two ships, the *Erebus* and the *Terror*, which had returned from a voyage of exploration in the Antarctic, and a crew of about a hundred and twenty, he sailed away—never to return. His fate was long a mystery, and many relief expeditions went out in search of him but only gradually did the facts come to light.

Franklin had cruised from Baffin Bay through Lancaster Sound into Barrow Strait. He had first turned northwards up Wellington Channel, and when stopped by the ice he had returned by a route he had himself discovered, between Cornwallis and Bathurst Islands into McDougall Bay.

Having wintered on Beechey Island he cruised southwards down Peel Sound, where he spent his second winter.

Here, however, he was misled by inaccurate maps: as they showed King William Island connected with

Boothia Land, he did not realize that between the two is a narrow channel, the James Ross Strait. He therefore tried to traverse Victoria Strait west of the island, and in this his ships were so irretrievably ice-bound that he had to abandon them.

The explorers then travelled overland, but soon a number of them died, among them Franklin himself. The survivors, gradually losing strength and hope, plodded on to the last: the Eskimos, who themselves were too short of food to help them, said that 'they fell and died as they walked'.

It was later found that Franklin, by turning south-wards from Lancaster Sound down Peel Sound, had entered on a practicable route through this maze of channels. Hence, Franklin is generally regarded as the discoverer of the North-West Passage; but it was many years before it was actually traversed—in 1905 by the Norwegian explorer Roald Amundsen. Amundsen also re-located the North Magnetic Pole, which is not fixed but has a gradual movement.

The discoveries north of Canada naturally revived interest in the idea of a North-East Passage. So little was known about conditions in this region that it was even thought there might be another large continent north of Siberia—until in 1879 G. W. de Long tried to reach it, but instead found only two small islands.

In 1878, after two preliminary investigations, the experienced Swedish explorer A. E. Nordenskiöld sailed in search of the Passage. At first he made good progress, and after only two months his ship, the *Vega*, was off Cape Chelyuskin, the most northerly point of Continental Asia. The explorers hoped that in spite of the fog they would reach Japan before the end of the year.

When they had reached a point only 120 miles from Bering Straits, however, their ship was frozen in. While wintering they made several dog-sledge expeditions overland, and they were greatly cheered by the friendliness of the Chuckchis, a people of North-East Siberia who somewhat resemble both the Red Indians and the Mongols.

Not until mid-July of the next year was the expedition able to proceed, but two days later it sighted East Cape. After calling at Japan, it sailed on south of India, through the Suez Canal, and so back to Sweden. It was thus the first not only to discover the North-East Passage, but also to circumnavigate the whole Eurasian landmass.

Gradually the great object of Arctic exploration ceased to be the North-West Passage, and became the North Pole. This seemed for a time almost inaccessible, until Elisha Kane of the U.S. Navy showed how it might be reached. During the quest for Franklin, Kane had discovered some hopeful-looking channels west of Greenland.

Attempts to reach the Pole by ship were unavailing, and so in 1893 the Norwegian explorer Fridjof Nansen tried an original and very hazardous method. Study of ice-drift in the Arctic suggested that he might use the currents to take him right across the Pole.

His vessel, the *Fram*, was specially constructed to resist the pressure of the ice, and north of the New Siberian Islands he deliberately let her be frozen in. Though the ice at one time threatened to crush her, it carried her northwards, but at about latitude 86° Nansen decided that it would be better to try to finish the journey by dog-sledges carrying kayaks (light Eskimo-type canoes).

He and his one companion, Johansen, at first made good progress, but the surface became too hummocky to make sledging possible, so they regretfully decided to abandon the venture and to make for Franz Josef Land, 450 miles away. By the time they reached it they were so short of food they had had to kill all but two of their sledge-dogs to feed the others; the ice was so thick that they could not hope for early rescue.

Only in the following summer, after spending their third winter in the Arctic, were they rescued by another expedition. This took them back to Norway, where they were rejoined by the *Fram*. Though they had not succeeded in reaching the Pole, they had shown that it is surrounded not by land but by sea, and they had accomplished the greatest of Arctic voyages. The *Fram* herself had reached further north than any other ship had ever gone, and what was called 'Nansen's Furthest North' was well beyond this.

In 1897 the Swedish engineer Andrée embarked on a venture even more hazardous than that of Nansen: with two companions he attempted to reach the Pole by balloon. After he soared from Spitzbergen, some of the buoys he dropped were recovered, and one of his carrier-pigeons reached home, but for years no more was heard of him. Only in 1930 were the remains of his camp discovered. His balloon had descended at about 83° north, and the balloonists had died while trying to return on foot across the ice.

The most determined of all the Arctic explorers was Robert Peary of the U.S. Navy. His duties took him to Central America, where he felt that the fame of Columbus, the first to discover that region, could be equalled in modern times only by that of the man who should first reach the North Pole. To be that man became the ambition of his life.

Having trained himself as an explorer in an unknown part of Greenland, in 1891 he led an expedition into its north. Though his leg was broken on the voyage out, he insisted on continuing the journey, and he and his only companion, Eivind Astrup, were the first to reach the northern coast of Greenland. This gained him the reputation of being the greatest dog-sledge traveller in the world.

He returned to that region several times, intending to use it as a base for reaching the Pole. His first attempts failed; all involved great hardship and peril, and on one journey he was crippled with frostbite so seriously that all his toes had to be amputated. Having learned to walk and use snow-shoes without them, he continued his work.

On his earlier expeditions Peary explored much of

Northern Greenland and the islands beyond, and he also found and brought back to America three great meteorites, one the largest in the world. Unlike the earlier explorers, he was able to make friends with the Eskimos and to win their confidence: he learned from them how best to live in the Arctic, and it was with their aid that his longer explorations were carried out. He also made improvements in the gear used by Arctic explorers.

Peary devised a method of organizing an expedition so efficient that it is now in general use. The explorers are divided into a number of groups: the task of the supporting parties is simply to blaze a trail and provide a number of store-depôts and then turn back. Thus they enable another small and very efficient party to make the final dash to the expedition's goal.

Early in 1909 Peary, with his negro servant and four Eskimos, made another attempt to reach the Pole, starting from Cape Columbia in Grant Land, north of Greenland. Weather conditions were unusually favourable, and his method of supporting parties worked admirably. This enabled him to make the double journey out and back in safety; and on his return to civilization the dramatic message was flashed across the world: 'Stars and Stripes nailed to the Pole'—and he had, in fact, on 6th April 1909 raised the flag of the United States above the snow-cairn he had built at the North Pole.

21 To the South Pole

So completely had Cook exploded the idea of an habitable land in the far south that for some time few attempts were made at exploring that region. Some American sealers and whalers reached islands unknown to the geographers, but they preferred to keep their discoveries to themselves.

In 1820 the Russian explorer Bellingshausen led an expedition into the southern seas. Much of his route lay nearer the Pole than that of Cook, and among his discoveries was Peter I Island, the first land to be discovered beyond the Antarctic Circle. About the same time Graham Land was discovered, but it is not certain who first sighted it; this important discovery—of a peninsula of the Antarctic Continent—is claimed both by Britain, for J. Bransfield, and by America. About that time, too, the British sealer J. Weddell entered what he called George IV Sea and is now called the Weddell Sea. Unfortunately, adverse winds prevented his going further south.

These and other discoveries revived interest in Antarctic exploration and a number of landfalls were made. In 1838 the French explorer Dumont d'Urville discovered Louis Phillippe Land south of Cape Horn; two years later he discovered Adele Land on the far side of the continent, just as not far away C. Wilkes of the U.S. Navy was discovering Wilkes Land.

The first vessels specially strengthened to resist ice-pressure in the Antarctic were two British ships, the *Erebus* and *Terror*. Their commander was the James Ross who had discovered the North Magnetic Pole.

Ross had become an authority on magnetism, and now, in 1840, his aim was to locate the corresponding southern Pole. Having set up magnetic observatories at the Cape of Good Hope and elsewhere, he chose a course to avoid the lands recently found by d'Urville and Wilkes.

Like them, he sighted an unknown shore, but he realized that it was not a large island but part of a southern continent hitherto unknown: Antarctica. To his surprise he observed in the distance mountains fourteen thousand feet high and he was still more amazed when he saw two volcanoes; he named these, after his ships, Mounts Erebus and Terror.

Like his predecessors Ross found it impossible to land on this continent, but with great difficulty he succeeded in raising the Union Flag on Possession Island nearby, claiming the adjoining coast, Victoria Land, for Britain. Moreover, his work greatly advanced the study of the earth's magnetism.

Again interest in this remote region faded; in fact, until 1874 no steamship crossed the Antarctic Circle.

This was then crossed by the British vessel *Challenger*, carrying out an important scientific research.

Not until 1893 was any landing made on the mainland of Antarctica; this was achieved by the Norwegian explorer C. A. Larsen. Included in the landing-party was C. E. Borchgrevink, of Norwegian and British parentage. Five years later, Borchgrevink commanded the first expedition to winter on the Antarctic Continent. In addition to making some short sledge journeys inland, he carried out some scientific investigations. Other research expeditions visited Antarctica during the first few years of the twentieth century.

The most important of these was made in 1901 by Robert Falcon Scott. His ship, the *Discovery*, was specially adapted for scientific work in the Antarctic, and among her other equipment was a captive balloon, from which inaccessible regions could be surveyed. She was frozen in for two years in the Ross Sea off Victoria Land; the explorers landed and erected their huts on King Edward VII Land.

From this base Scott, with E. H. Shackleton and Edward Wilson, made a long dog-sledge expedition to the south. They had to face unforeseeable difficulties, for travel across Antarctica is more perilous even than it is in the Arctic.

Because part of Antarctica's surface is high above sea-level, the cold is much more intense and the risk of frostbite much greater; there is an almost complete absence of animal life; the surface varies from loose snow to hard narrow ridges very destructive to the sledge-runners; deep crevasses abound, some of them masked by a thin covering of snow; a confusing mist, the white-out, may hide everything from sight. The low altitude of the sun makes it difficult to take bearings; there is no bright Pole Star to indicate the south; and the proximity of the Magnetic Pole reduces the reliability of the compass.

In spite of these difficulties, and though the death of their dogs meant that they themselves had to haul the sledges, the explorers made good progress, reaching a point nearly four hundred miles from their base, less than 8° from the Pole. Here a blizzard forced them to turn back; food ran short, and they were afflicted by scurvy. After they had experienced great hardship, the sight of Mount Erebus showed them that their depôt was only a hundred miles away, and the last of their store-depôts provided them with enough food to reach it.

They had covered over nine hundred and fifty miles at an average rate of about ten miles a day, and their journey, with another which Scott made next year, disclosed much information about the interior of Antarctica, with its great inland Polar Plateau nearly ten thousand feet high. The explorers had advanced science and had gained much information about the special needs of Antarctic travel. This was very helpful to other explorers, German, French, Swedish, and British, who later visited the continent.

Though after his arduous sledge journey Shackleton

had had to be invalided home, he returned to Antarctica, in the *Nimrod*, in 1907. Among the achievements of the expedition which he led were the ascent of Mount Erebus, an active volcano 13,700 feet high, and the discovery of the South Magnetic Pole, at 72° 25' south, 155°16' east, by T. W. E. David and Douglas Mawson.

In October 1908 Shackleton, with three companions, their sledges hauled not by dogs but by Manchurian ponies, attempted to reach the South Pole.

They were aided by good weather, and within a month they had gone further than the previous expedition. Unfortunately their ponies suffered so badly from the hardships of the journey that three of them had to be shot; the other fell down a crevasse and was lost, though the sledge was saved. As before, blizzards held the explorers up, and shortage of food forced them to turn back. On the return journey they had so little food that they had to eat the flesh of the dead ponies, and this brought on grave illness. They reached the *Nimrod* just in time for her to sail home before winter closed in.

They had not reached the South Pole, but they had got within two degrees of it, about ninety-seven miles, and there they had raised the British flag. They had shown, too, that with good organization and ample supplies it should be possible to reach the Pole.

Scott's second expedition to the Antarctic, like that of Shackleton, combined scientific work with an attempt to reach the South Pole. Even the outward journey was hazardous, for his ship, the *Terra Nova*, found it difficult to force her way through the ice and was imperilled by a storm. The landing was made and scientific research begun in January 1911; Scott's journey towards the Pole was not to start until the following November, but before then he received disconcerting news.

A Norwegian boy, Roald Amundsen, had made up his mind to devote his life to exploration. Believing that an explorer ought to be able to command his own vessel, he went to sea to get his training, and served as mate in the *Belgica* when she visited the Antarctic.

His original aim, like that of Peary, was to discover the North Pole. In a small fishing-smack, the *Gjoa*, he was the first, in 1903, to traverse the North-West Passage, and during the voyage he rediscovered the North Magnetic Pole.

Some years later Amundsen bought the *Fram*, intending, as Nansen had done, to let her freeze in and be carried by the Arctic currents so near to the Pole that he could attempt to reach it across the ice. But when, in 1909, he learned that Peary had been ahead of him, he decided to change his plans and make instead for the South Pole.

His experience had made him realize the value of sledge-dogs for polar exploration, and he made his base not on the edge of the Antarctic Continent but in the Bay of Whales in the Ross Sea. He made his first attempt to reach the Pole in September 1911, but some of his companions were so badly attacked by frostbite, and even some of the dogs felt the cold so much, that he had to return.

By 20th October, when he made his second attempt, the weather had become much milder—too warm, indeed, for men who had to toil up the long glacier from the Ice-Barrier almost at sea-level to the high Polar Plateau. Though on the Plateau they were held up by a blizzard, and though they encountered great peril when crossing a glacier badly broken by crevasses, they made very good progress. They were careful to mark their trail in readiness for the return journey, some of their markers consisting of dried fish stuck in the snow.

The dogs worked splendidly, and Amundsen's men were skilled in handling them. As the load they had to draw lessened, some of the sledge-dogs were slaughtered and served as food not only for the other dogs but for the men. If a dog happened to fall through a crust of ice covering a crevasse, it was easy to haul him out. One dog, however, fell through a crust on what seemed solid ice below, but when one of the men jumped down to rescue him, he found it was only a second crust which collapsed beneath his feet; only his grip on the sledge-harness saved him from falling into the gulf.

After passing the most southerly point attained by Shackleton two years before, they flew a Norwegian flag in triumph on their leading sledge. Another week's travel brought them to the Pole, but to make quite certain they had actually reached it they made a number of short sledge-journeys in different directions.

Yet Amundsen was not fully satisfied. Like Peary, he had set his heart on being the first to reach the North Pole—and instead he had been first to reach the South.

His expedition returned safely to their base, after having first marked the discovery on 14th December 1911 of the South Pole by erecting above it a small tent above which fluttered the flag of Norway and the pendant of the *Fram*.

Greatly as he hoped to be the first to reach the Pole, Scott was not going to let Amundsen's attempt spur him into a mere race for priority; he had his scientific work to carry out. So it was not until the 2nd of November, a week later than Amundsen's, that his expedition headed for the Pole. He had further to travel, too, for his base was not on the ice of the Ross Sea, but on the land; and here the weather was far less favourable.

Unlike Amundsen, he was using not only dogs, but also ponies and motor-sledges, and these proved disappointing. Though the motors at first worked well, their engines overheated and they had to be abandoned; and, as planned, the ponies were killed to feed the dogs and men. The appalling weather made progress slow, a blizzard held it up for several days, the soft snow was difficult to cross, and the glare of the sunshine on the white surface made some of the party suffer badly from snow-blindness.

At the foot of the glacier leading up to the Polar Plateau the dog-teams were sent back, and three teams of four men each hauled their heavily-laden sledges up to the Plateau. It was laborious work, and the explorers began to tire; there were several falls into the crevasses, and one man found himself suspended by his harness over an eighty-foot drop. Only with difficulty could the others rescue him.

The two supporting teams turned back, one after the other, and on the return journey they met with many difficulties and dangers. One of the teams saved much time by tobogganing hundreds of feet down a glacier, but even so they ran short of food and were so badly afflicted by scurvy that when at last they neared the end of their journey they could go no further and had to be rescued by dog-teams sent out from their base.

Here the explorers waited with growing anxiety for Scott and his companions to return, but when the winter closed in they knew their comrades must have perished. Nothing could be done till next summer, and then a search-party set out along their trail. Presently they found a tent buried in the snow, and in it were three dead bodies, some letters, and Captain Scott's diary. They took the diary and the letters away, but they left the bodies in the tent and heaped up over it a cairn of snow.

The diary explained what had happened. Scott, with his four companions—Wilson, Captain Oates, Bowers, and Evans—had at first made good progress, then again a blizzard delayed them. Because of the condition of the snow, it needed tremendous effort to cover ten miles a day. Scott noticed uneasily that even when the temperature was a little milder than usual they still felt cold; this was a sign that they were getting exhausted.

When they were within two days' march of the Pole, they saw in the distance a black speck on the snow, and they knew that this could be nothing natural. They found it was a flag tied to a sledge-bearer, and nearby were traces of a camp, with many tracks and paw-marks in the snow. They realized with dismay that the Norwegians had been ahead of them.

On 17th January they arrived at the tent, with its flags, which Amundsen had left to mark the Pole; within the tent was a letter addressed to Captain Scott, wishing him good fortune on the journey home. Next day, weary and downcast, they faced that long hazardous journey, but first they raised the British flag alongside the Norwegian at the South Pole.

Although, aided by a southerly wind, they crossed the Plateau fairly quickly, Scott's entries in his diary show the anxiety he felt about his companions' health; Evans was very seriously blistered. While going down the glacier they were badly hindered by the crevasses, and were in danger of running short of food.

The depôt on the glacier enabled them to replenish their stores, but now none of them was in good condition. Evans got worse and worse; he was suffering not only from blisters, but from concussion of the brain caused by a fall. At last he collapsed and died in the snow.

When the survivors reached a store-depôt on the Ice-Barrier below the glacier they were horrified to find that much of the fuel-oil had evaporated. This meant that they would be unable not only to warm their tent, but even to cook enough hot meals and melt enough snow to obtain drinking water—and without hot meals and hot drinks life in the Antarctic is impossible.

To make things worse, the weather down on the Barrier was unexpectedly cold. Fuel ran so short that the explorers had barely enough to warm their food; this weakened them so that the slightest task became an effort, and their speed was reduced to about five miles a day.

Oates especially suffered from frostbite, and could do little more than limp along. Knowing that the others could go on faster without him, he asked them to leave him; and when they refused he deliberately left his tent to die in the blizzard—'the act,' Scott wrote in his diary, 'of a very gallant gentleman.'

The others were able to travel more easily without him, and at last they managed to get within eleven miles of a depôt where they would have found plenty of food and fuel. There was just a chance they might be able to reach it, but a raging blizzard made travel impossible. For eight days they remained in their tent, using up their last supplies; every day they prepared to start, but when they looked outside they saw nothing but the whirling snowdrifts.

'I do not think we can hope for better things now,' Scott wrote in his diary on 28th March 1912. 'We shall stick it out to the end, but we are getting weaker, of course, and the end cannot be far.

G

'It seems a pity, but I do not think I can write more. . . .'

'Had we lived,' runs another entry in his diary, 'I should have had a tale of the hardihood, endurance, and courage of my companions, which would have stirred the heart of every Englishman. These rough notes and our dead bodies must tell the tale.'

22 Mountain and Cave; Sea and Air

MODERN exploration gets much help from science and invention. Portable radio-sets enable an expedition to keep in touch with its base and if necessary to appeal for help; 'walky-talky' sets enable its members to keep in touch with one another. Tape-recorder and ciné-camera enable it to make permanent records of the scenes it visits and the animals or peoples it encounters. Helicopters and other aircraft can aid it by an advance reconnaissance, watch its progress from above, and drop supplies by parachute. Improvements in gear, in medicine, and even in diet, make its work less uncertain and hazardous: the weakness which overcame Scott and his comrades as they returned from the Pole may possibly have been due to lack of some essential vitamin in their food.

Expeditions may be sent to remote places in search of the oil or the other minerals so essential in peace and war—including, of course, uranium. These are found by ingenious apparatus which discloses conditions under the ground: explosives and microphones for producing 'seismic shocks' (artificial earthquakes), electrical appliances for detecting metallic ores, and instruments which show the slightest local variations in the earth's gravitational pull.

Mountaineering became a sport when the Wetter-horn, in Switzerland, was climbed in 1854; but long before that it was a form of scientific exploration. Mont Blanc was in fact first climbed, in 1786, to aid the French geologist, H. B. de Saussure, in his researches on mountain structure. Later, de Saussure climbed it himself.

Climbs of exploration followed in other parts of the Alps, and then in the earth's other mountain ranges, the loftiest of which is the Himalayas. When these were being surveyed in 1852, a technician excitedly announced that the calculations showed one peak slightly overtopping the others. As its poetical Tibetan name, Chomolunga ('Goddess Mother of the World'), was not then known, this, the highest mountain of earth, was called, after the Director of the Survey, Mount Everest.

Needless to say, it has long attracted mountaineers, but until recently their attempts to climb it ended in failure, and some of them in tragedy. In 1933 aircraft flights were made over it, obtaining information very useful in latter attempts to climb it.

The British Everest Expedition, 1953, profited from this, and from the very latest improvements in mountaineering technique and gear, when, under the leadership of John Hunt, it attempted the ascent of Mount

Everest from Nepal. Its route led up a long glacier, the Western Cwm: in this lies a great ice-fall, where a change in the level of the valley-floor makes the ice slope steeply. It is strewn with immense blocks and furrowed with deep crevasses, while movements of the ice may overturn the blocks or widen a crevasse, or open a new crevasse, without the slightest warning. In one place the ice is almost continuously in motion.

Beyond the ice-fall the glacier leads to the base of a precipitous slope, almost a mile high, the Lhotse Face. With great difficulty in that thin air, the expedition succeeded not only in surmounting this but also man-handling their equipment up to the South Col above. From this the actual attempts were made to reach the highest point of Mount Everest. The 'first assault' had to turn back, but it succeeded in reaching a slightly lower peak, South Summit, which had never before been climbed.

This prepared the way for the 'second assault' on Everest, made by the New Zealander Edmund Hillary, accompanied by the Sherpa (native hillman) Tenzing. Having camped for the night alone on the bleak mountain-top, and starting out at dawn, they reached and passed South Summit and crossed the untrodden South-East Ridge beyond. Progress was very difficult, and involved a hazardous climb over a great boulder; in that bitter air their breath froze and threatened to clog the outlets of their oxygen apparatus. But on 29th May 1953 they achieved their ambition and returned safely after raising above earth's highest mountain the flags of their own countries, of India, and of the United Nations.

Caves have always had a strange fascination, but until modern times they were shunned as fearsome or 'taboo'—or both. Now their exploration forms at once a hazardous sport, 'mountaineering in reverse', and the science of Spelæology. One of the first to study it was the great French eighteenth-century naturalist, Cuvier.

Many important caves were discovered by accident. The Mammoth Caves of Kentucky, the largest so far known, were found in 1809 by the American trapper Hutchins, when he was trailing a wounded bear. In 1901 a Texan cowboy, Jim White, was startled to see what he thought was the smoke of a volcano; it was an immense swarm of bats emerging from another large American cave at Carlsbad. In 1940 five French boys, while rescuing their dog from a hole into which it had fallen, discovered the cave of Lascaux in the Dordogne, its walls decorated with strange animal paintings.

Such Painted Caves were already well known, and the discovery of the first of these decorations had also been accidental. In 1875 the Spanish archæologist Marcelino de Sautuola was searching for flint implements on the floor of a cavern at Altamira when he was startled to hear his small daughter shouting something about bulls. Looking up, he saw that the cavern roof was decorated with paintings of bison and other animals. The origin of these was for a time doubtful, but a thin film of calcite covering some of them showed that they must be very old, and it is now agreed that they were made, possibly ten thousand years ago, by prehistoric man.

Discoveries are still being made in caves, which provide the only form of exploration possible in our islands. But amateur spelæologists should only attempt cave-exploration under experienced leadership, for it can be very dangerous. Recently a young 'caver' got irretrievably wedged in a rock cranny, where he perished in spite of heroic efforts to rescue him.

Until fairly-modern times the ocean-depths could be studied only from the surface by such methods as sounding-apparatus, self-registering thermometers, devices for sampling the water at various depths and ooze from the sea-floor. These were the methods used by Cook, d'Urville, and Ross. In the early-nineteenth century the Russians made voyages for research in oceanography, and this was also carried out by Darwin during his cruise with Fitzroy in the *Beagle*.

The *Challenger* expedition of 1872–6 studied a wide variety of subjects. It experimented on the variation of the compass; charted the sea-floor; measured the temperature of the water at various levels; ascertained the exact bearings, hitherto uncertain, of many islands and reefs; estimated the strength and direction of the currents; and investigated the natural history of the sea and the formation of coral-reefs.

The diving-bell and the older forms of diving-dress could be used only for fairly short distances under water.

The deep-sea-diving-outfit, made of steel and aluminium, enables the explorer to go over five hundred feet down, and in his bathysphere the American naturalist, C. W. Beebe, attained a depth of half a mile.

Beebe's pioneer work of deep-sea exploration was followed up in 1947 when the Swiss physicist Auguste Piccard, using a ten-ton bathyscaphe, reached a depth of nearly two miles. In 1959 his son, Jacques Piccard, and Andreas Rechnitzer, in their seventy-five-ton bathyscaphe the *Trieste*, explored a gulf in the Pacific at a depth of three and a half miles.

From the surface the depth of the sea has long been estimated by 'sounding the lead'; in the old days by hand, in modern times by sounding-machines. In really deep water this is a lengthy task, but the echo-sounding apparatus, which records the 'reflection' from the sea-floor of ultra-sonic waves, can be used continuously while a ship is under way.

Specimens of the sea-floor have been obtained and information about the structure of the sea-bed is gained by instruments similar to those used on land for studying local variations in the earth's magnetism and gravitational pull. In spite of such methods, we know less about conditions below the oceans than we do about those on the moon; in their depths there may be creatures long thought to be completely extinct, as well as valuable mineral ores.

The atmosphere is studied both on the ground and high aloft by means of meteorological instruments. One of the most important is the barometer, which measures the air's pressure; it was invented in 1643 by the Italian physicist Torricelli. In the same century the French philosopher Blaise Pascal, by taking a barometer up a mountain and aloft in a balloon, showed that the atmospheric pressure falls as the distance above sea-level increases. Aircraft with pressurized cabins and balloons with air-tight gondolas have taken their crews high above the ground. In 1932 Auguste Piccard was taken by a balloon to a height of over fifty-five thousand feet.

Many other methods are used to study conditions in the upper air. On the ground meteorological observatories and smaller weather stations record the readings of a number of instruments and these are studied and charted on an international basis. A number of Ocean Weather Ships make observations far out to sea, and specially-equipped aircraft carry out regular 'Met' (meteorological) flights as various levels.

The weather ships and some of the land stations also investigate conditions in the upper air by means of the radio-sonde. This consists of a small balloon carrying a number of instruments together with a small radio-transmitter by which their readings are flashed to earth. Its flight can meanwhile be followed not only by telescopes, but also by radio or radar direction-finders. With the radio-sonde, and its improved form the radar-sonde, conditions can be investigated at heights of over one hundred thousand feet, and rockets take recording instruments over a hundred miles high.

Rockets have also been used very successfully for such

G*

purposes as to launch the artificial satellites. Though one purpose of these is to get information with a view to preparing the way for space travel, they are also used to study conditions at high altitudes and to take 'long shots' of the earth.

23 Across the Poles

AIRCRAFT soon showed their value in Polar exploration. In 1925 Richard Evelyn Byrd, of the U.S. Navy, flew with one companion over the North Pole. Here the only great difficulties were to land his monoplane, the *Josephine Ford*, on Spitzbergen and to get her off the ground. Once she was airborne, the journey to the Pole and back was accomplished with surprising ease.

Amundsen had hoped to be the first to fly over the Pole, but he did not make his attempt until after Byrd's return. Then, with the Italian aircraft-designer Umberto Nobile, he crossed the Arctic, from Spitzbergen over the Pole to Alaska, in the dirigible *Norge*. In 1926 Nobile made a second flight over the Pole, but on the return journey his dirigible, the *Italia*, made a forced landing; he was seriously injured and was rescued only with difficulty. Amundsen and his pilot lost their lives while flying out in a seaplane to help in the rescue.

Having flown over the North Pole, Byrd decided to attempt a similar achievement in the south. Here much work had been done since the tragic end of Scott's expedition. In 1911 Mawson, the discoverer of the South Magnetic Pole, led another scientific expedition into the Antarctic. While he was carrying out an exploration inland two of his companions were killed, and he himself fell into a crevasse from which he had the greatest difficulty in climbing out.

The first attempt to cross the Antarctic Continent was made by Shackleton in 1914. He was unable even to land, however, for his ship, the *Endurance*, was crushed in the ice. After camping on the floes until they broke up, he and his crew managed to reach Elephant Island by boat. Realizing that it was impossible for them all to reach civilization, he sailed off with five others to bring them help. When, after a hazardous voyage of over eight hundred miles in an open boat, he landed on South Georgia, he had to make another equally hazardous journey across a range of uncharted mountains to reach a settlement on the far side of the island. After four months on Elephant Island his men were rescued, but in Antarctica, not realizing what had happened, his supporting party had prepared a supply depôt for him, in conditions so arduous that three of its members were killed.

Byrd, when he led an expedition to Antarctica in 1928, had plans more far-reaching than a mere flight to and from the Pole; his chief aim was to explore the continent over the surface and by air. His base, Little America, was large and well equipped, with radio-masts, an aircraft hangar, a garage for his 'snow-mobile', and a gymnasium to keep his men fit. From this he sent out a number of surface expeditions and made several flights. By one of these he rescued his geologists after their aircraft had crashed.

His flight over the South Pole was by no means so easy as that over the North, for he had first to soar high enough to cross the Central Plateau. Finding that his aircraft, the *Floyd Bennett*, was too heavily laden to gain enough height, and that he would either have to dump some of his fuel, which would mean turning back, or throw overboard the food he would need if a forced landing made him return on foot, he decided to sacrifice the food. Thus he was able to complete his journey, over the Pole and back to base. His expedition gained much information about parts of Antarctica hitherto unexplored.

The second Byrd Antarctic Expedition of 1934 aimed not at reaching the Pole, but at carrying out further exploration from Little America. Its work included the setting up, a hundred miles further south, of a Weather Advance Station, where one observer was to spend the winter. Feeling that he could not ask anyone else to carry out so lonely and perilous a task, Byrd undertook it himself. When after several months' duty he was

relieved, he was seriously ill, poisoned by carbon monoxide from a defective stove. But his work, and that of
the other members of the expedition, had been satisfactorily carried out.

Byrd's three further visits to Antarctica included two
flights over the South Pole. On the third of these his
object was to find a suitable landing-strip for a base to
be set up in the heart of the Antarctic Continent, the
Amundsen-Scott South Pole Station.

This Station was established as part of the programme
of the International Geophysical Year 1957–8. In this
the scientists of many nations co-operated in studying
the earth and the forces which act upon it; their work
included a number of explorations in Antarctica.

The most ambitious of these was the Commonwealth
Trans-Antarctic Expedition, 1955. Its leader, Dr.
Vivian Fuchs, would attempt to cross the continent
from Weddell Sea to Ross Sea; Hillary, who had
ascended Mount Everest, would simultaneously journey
from Ross Sea towards the Pole, setting up a series of
supply depôts for Dr. Fuchs to use during the second
half of his journey. The purpose of both parties, and of
the other members of the expedition, was to carry out a
number of scientific investigations on the Antarctic ice-
cap.

Early in 1956 the expedition set up its base camp,
Shackleton Base, on the shores of Weddell Sea. Here an
advance party wintered, later to be joined by their
comrades under Dr. Fuchs. He organized a number of

explorations, and established an Advance Depôt, South Ice, two hundred and fifty miles nearer the Pole. In this lonely spot three men spent the following winter, studying the weather and the formation of the ice at various depths below the surface.

The party led by Hillary had meanwhile landed on the far side of Antarctica, where it had established Scott Base on McMurdo Sound in the Ross Sea. The investigations it carried out included a study of life in the off-shore waters.

The work of all these explorers, in cold so intense, was painful as well as laborious. It produced important results, but at the same time it was subsidiary to their main task, which was to carry out the two Polar journeys.

The expedition led by Hillary left Scott Base on 14th October 1957. Well equipped as it was with dog-teams and tractors, it found the climb up to the Polar Plateau so difficult that a month was needed to accomplish it. On the Plateau the air was so thin that the heavily-laden tractors could move only with difficulty; at times it seemed that the whole attempt to establish the depôts would have to be abandoned.

After much effort, however, the journey continued and the store depôts were set up as planned. Although this was not part of his programme, Hillary then decided to push on to the Pole so as to map out a route for Dr. Fuchs to follow. By the time he had sighted the Amundsen-Scott South Pole Station, where the Americans welcomed him heartily, he had almost run out of fuel.

Dr. Fuch's expedition did not leave Shackleton Base until 24th November, and it too encountered almost insuperable difficulties. Though it was equipped not only with tractors but with 'Sno-cats' the size of caravans, and although it at first crossed a region already traversed, not until 21st December did it reach South Ice. Here a halt was made for necessary repairs, but on Christmas Day the expedition was again on its way towards the Pole.

This was the most difficult part of the journey, for this region was completely unknown. As they travelled, the explorers systematically studied conditions in the ice, boring into it to get specimens from beneath the surface and producing small 'ice-quakes' by seismic shocks to ascertain conditions further below. This work, and the difficulties of travel, delayed them seriously, and when at last they arrived at the Pole, on 19th January 1958, they were exhausted. They were cheered by the welcome the Americans gave them, and by the opportunity for much-needed rest and refreshment.

Late though they were on schedule, Dr. Fuchs decided to complete the journey to Scott Base, over a thousand miles away. Again they encountered the usual difficulties and mishaps of Polar travel, and now came an accident which almost ended fatally. One of the explorers was almost poisoned by carbon monoxide from a leaking exhaust pipe, but oxygen from the welding apparatus saved his life.

On this part of the journey, however, the explorers could make better time, for they were now able to profit by Hillary's crossing of the region and by the store depôts he had set up. Now, too, they did not need to study the ice, for this had already been done. Nonetheless, conditions still made travel difficult, the descent from Polar Plateau being especially hazardous.

At last they sighted two landmarks, first Mounts Erebus and Terror, and then the cross erected on Observation Hill in memory of Captain Scott. Escorts from Scott Base and from an American base nearby came to welcome them, and by 2nd March 1958 they had succeeded in traversing the Antarctic Continent from coast to coast.

The next great Polar expedition was carried out in the Arctic. It had already been attempted in 1931 by the British explorer Hubert Wilkins: by fitting the deck of a submarine, the *Nautilus*, with ski-like runners to slide along the lower surface of the ice, by boring through it with large drills, and by surfacing in the wide leads, he had hoped to be able to travel under the sea to the North Pole. Though it gained useful information on Arctic conditions, the attempt proved quite impracticable.

But now, after more than twenty years later, the very latest developments in science and invention came to the explorers' aid. Where an ordinary submarine was bound to fail, a nuclear-powered submarine might hope to succeed. That submarine, commanded by William R. Anderson of the U.S. Navy, was also named the *Nautilus*, after the vessel in Jules Verne's

famous science-fiction story. She had already shown that
she could remain submerged far longer than the older
types of submarine, and in many other ways she was
more suited for such a venture. She was equipped with
special navigational devices, and with a fathometer for
showing her distance below the under-surface of the ice.

On her first attempt, in 1957, she entered the Arctic
between Greenland and Spitzbergen, but beyond 87°,
about one hundred and eighty miles from the Pole,
equipment failures forced her to turn back. Her second
attempt was made through the Bering Straits. Finding
the ice west of St. Lawrence Island too thick to pass,
she tried again east of the island. Here she got through
the Straits, but off the coast of Alaska, when only
twenty feet above the sea-floor, she encountered a
ridge of ice which extended to eighty-five feet below
sea-level—she cleared it only by a few feet! As the sea
beyond was shallower and the ice-sheet might be even
thicker, her commander reluctantly gave orders to
turn back.

When the *Nautilus* again returned to the Arctic, late
in July, she was equipped with a television set whose
upward-pointing lens enabled her crew to see the lower
surface of the ice. This had thinned so much that she
was now able to enter the Bering Straits west of St.
Lawrence Island. Further north it was still so thick,
however, that only a deep channel in the sea-floor, the
Barrow Sea Valley, enabled her to pass beneath it.

She headed northwards along this channel. For a time
the sea was about twelve thousand feet deep, but sud-

denly its depth was reduced to about three thousand feet. Then it deepened again; for about seventy miles the *Nautilus* had been passing over a submerged mountain range.

When, after more than sixty hours under water, she was approaching the Pole, the Commander asked her crew to observe the actual crossing by a moment of silent prayer. At 11.15 p.m. on 3rd August 1958 the North Pole was 'pierced'. Here the sea is 13,410 feet deep; it was at a temperature of just over 32°, and so thick was the ice that it formed a ridge extending to twenty-five feet below sea-level.

Even with the best equipment, submarine navigation near the Pole is so difficult that not until the *Nautilus* was able to surface could her crew be certain that she was on course. Bearings taken off Greenland showed that she was, and she cruised on to England.

This voyage, and another carried out some weeks later to and from the Pole by another U.S. nuclear-powered submarine, the *Skate*, shows that large cargo-carrying submarines might be able to travel submerged beneath the Arctic. They would then be following a route akin to that attempted three centuries before by Hudson and far more practicable than the long-sought North-East and North-West Passages, reaching the Far East from the seaports of the Atlantic by way of the North Pole.

24 Into Space

THE idea of space travel dates back to the second century A.D., when the Greek writer Lucian wrote what he called a *True History*, a very untrue adventure story about a voyage to the moon and a battle between its inhabitants and the sun's. Needless to say, he did not mean it to be taken seriously!

In the seventeenth century the great astronomer Kepler wrote another moon-voyage story. Though its Latin title, *Somnium*, means 'in sleep', Kepler based it partly on the science of his time. Another idea which he took seriously was that of interplanetary warfare; he wondered what sort of creatures might dwell on the other planets, and whether they or ourselves were the true 'Lords of the World'.

The moon could then be observed more effectively than ever before: in 1609 Galileo, using his newly-invented telescope, studied and sketched its surface. He was surprised to find it covered with mountain peaks and ranges, rings like volcanic craters, and dark patches which are really barren plains but which looked to him like 'seas'. Since then, the moon's surface has been studied more carefully, and mapped in detail.

Many other moon-travel stories have been written, the first really serious one being Jules Verne's *From the Earth to the Moon* (1865). Several suggestions have been made for actually reaching the moon, in spite of its distance, about two hundred and forty thousand miles; because of the absence of air between earth and moon, ordinary aircraft could never reach it.

Space can at present be explored only by the use of powerful rockets built in several stages. The first stages merely carry other smaller rockets and discharge them high in the air; the last stage, which is comparatively small, contains scientific instruments for recording conditions far above the ground, with radio apparatus for transmitting their readings. Each rocket, when it reaches the top of its flight, falls earthwards and is burned up by the resistance of the air.

These rockets have attained very great heights and transmitted valuable information regarding conditions in the upper air. In November 1956 a United States rocket, launched from a balloon nearly one hundred thousand feet above the Pacific, reached a height of four thousand miles.

The work of the International Geophysical Year involved using such rockets to carry artificial satellites high above the atmosphere. These contain scientific instruments which automatically transmit their recordings by radio. They travel very rapidly round the earth, not in circles but in ellipses which alternately bring them earthwards and then take them further away, but the resistance of the air first slows them so that they gradually spiral downwards and then destroys them.

Naturally there was keen rivalry between the only two nations wealthy enough to make such very costly experiments, the United States and Soviet Russia. The first artificial satellite to be successfully launched, on 4th October 1957, was the Russian *Sputnik* ('Satellite') *I*. A sphere almost two feet across and weighing 184 pounds, it began by travelling round the earth in an ellipse ranging from 500 to 120 miles, and it lasted ninety-two days.

Sputnik II, launched a month later, was far larger, weighing over 1100 pounds and being nearly six feet long; its greatest distance from the earth was about 900 miles and it lasted 161 days. In addition to scientific apparatus it carried a passenger, a husky dog, Laika, with apparatus for feeding her and supplying her with air, for recording her breathing, temperature, heart-beat, and so forth—and for killing her painlessly when the experiment was over.

The first United States artificial satellite, *Explorer I*, was a 30-pound cylinder, 80 inches long and 6 inches across. Launched on 1st February 1958, its original orbit ranged from about 200 to about 1370 miles from the earth, and it is expected to keep in flight for four years. Smaller, but reaching a greater height, over 2100 miles, was the United States *Vanguard I*, a 6-inch sphere weighing 3¼ pounds; it may last for 100 years from its date of launching, in March 1958.

Since then several other artificial satellites have been

sent aloft, by both Soviet Russia and the United States. Until recently the largest was the Russian *Sputnik III*, a cone 12 feet long, nearly 7 feet at its base, weighing 2926 pounds, and reaching a height of over 1000 miles. The satellites have obtained information on such subjects as the air's temperature and pressure at different heights, the earth's gravitation and magnetic and electrical conditions, the sun's radiation, the cosmic rays which arrive from outer space, and the small grains of drifting dust called micrometeors. The American *Vanguard II*, a 20-inch sphere launched in February 1959 to a height of 1790 miles, also carried a 'weather eye' for studying cloud formation from far aloft.

Some of the satellites have been seen, looking like stars moving across the sky. Their signals have been picked up by radio equipment, and some of them have been broadcast on the wireless. The United States satellite *Atlas*—also called *Score* ('Signal Communication Orbit Relay Experiment')—launched on 18th December 1958, broadcast a Christmas greeting from President Eisenhower: 'My message is a simple one. Through this unique means I convey to you and to all mankind America's wish for peace on earth and goodwill towards men everywhere.'

A rocket given the 'escape velocity' of about seven miles a second needed to overcome the earth's gravitational pull, can be sent into outer space. This speed has now been attained, and several rockets have been launched towards the moon.

The earliest recorded attempts to launch a lunar probe were made in 1958 by the United States. On the first attempt, *Moon Probe I* exploded, owing to some failure in its highly-complicated mechanism, after a flight of 77 seconds. *Pioneer I*, launched on 11th October, failed to reach the moon, but travelled over 70,000 miles before its power failed and it began to fall back. *Pioneer II* failed to ignite, but *Pioneer III*, launched on 6th December, reached a height of about 63,000 miles.

Though not one of the probes succeeded in reaching its objective, they gained much information about conditions at great heights, its instruments transmitting observations on zones of radiation around the earth, on its magnetism, and on micrometeors.

The attempts made during 1959 were much more successful. *Pioneer IV*, launched on 3rd March, succeeded in getting within 37,000 miles of the moon, afterwards becoming a minor planet forever travelling in an elliptical course round the sun. The observations it made included not only radiation in space but an attempted measurement of the moon's light.

Remarkable as this achievement was, the Russians had already surpassed it. Their *Lunik I*, launched on 2nd January, and weighing about 800 pounds, got within 4,000 miles of the moon before journeying on to become an artificial minor planet. It likewise collected valuable information, and at one point on its flight it ejected a cloud of sodium vapour, telescopically visible from the earth.

Lunik II, launched on 12th September, actually hit

the moon, after a flight lasting 36 hours. It was slightly heavier than *Lunik I*, and it too ejected a cloud of sodium vapour during its flight.

Even more remarkable was the flight of *Lunik III*. Launched on 4th October, it travelled beyond the moon, circled round on its far side, and returned earthwards, then adopting an elliptical course which alternately brings it within about 25,000 miles of the earth and takes it nearly 300,000 miles away. It was expected to keep on course for about six months before it either comes within the earth's atmosphere and burns up, or else collides with the moon. Unfortunately, contact with it was lost, due to the failure of its radio transmitters.

At one end of its cylindrical body, *Lunik III* carried a photo-electric cell, so arranged that when it got on the far side of the moon it would face towards the sun. In this position its other end was then directed towards the moon, and a camera took a photograph of its surface; the photograph was then processed and televised to earth.

The moon always keeps practically the same face turned towards the earth, so that its rear part, about three-sevenths of its whole surface, is for ever hidden from our sight. *Lunik III* had successfully taken a photograph of the greater part of this hidden portion, and its details are now being eagerly studied by astronomers all over the world. The Russians are now using the explorers' right of naming these newly discovered features.

During 1960 several interesting launchings were

made. The United States *Pioneer V*, carried high above the earth by rocket and then launched into space by a signal from the Jodrell Bank radio, was directed towards the sun. It was intended to intersect the orbit of Venus, and though it failed to do so, it got within 7,000,000 miles of that orbit, and will travel round the sun once in about 311 days, in an elongated ellipse. To conserve its power, its radio apparatus was switched on and off at intervals by signal from Jodrell Bank, and its equipment was arranged to investigate the intensity of magnetism and the cosmic rays, the occurrence of micrometeors, the possibility that clouds of particles may exist in interplanetary space, and the cause of the Zodiacal light.

The American *Tiros I*, launched in April 1960, was a meteorological satellite, intended to investigate cloud formations by means of sun-powered telecameras and infra-red equipment. In the same month the U.S. launched its satellite *Transit I B*, intended as an aid to ocean navigation.

So large was the satellite launched by the Russians in May 1960 that they deny that it is a satellite at all: they say that it is really an unmanned space-ship intended to pave the way for launching a manned vehicle for flight into interplanetary space.

This may well be accomplished in the near future, and it should be a hope that such an achievement will transcend national rivalries, that all the nations of earth will unite in one great international attempt to achieve the exploration of space.

Index